**Only a Black Athlete
Can Save Us Now**

Forerunners: Ideas First

Short books of thought-in-process scholarship, where intense
analysis, questioning, and speculation take the lead

FROM THE UNIVERSITY OF MINNESOTA PRESS

Grant Farred
Only a Black Athlete Can Save Us Now

Anna Watkins Fisher
Safety Orange

Heather Warren-Crow and Andrea Jonsson
Young-Girls in Echoland: #Theorizing Tiqqun

Joshua Schuster and Derek Woods
Calamity Theory: Three Critiques of Existential Risk

Daniel Bertrand Monk and Andrew Herscher
**The Global Shelter Imaginary: IKEA Humanitarianism
and Rightless Relief**

Catherine Liu
Virtue Hoarders: The Case against the Professional Managerial Class

Christopher Schaberg
Grounded: Perpetual Flight . . . and Then the Pandemic

Marquis Bey
The Problem of the Negro as a Problem for Gender

Cristina Beltrán
Cruelty as Citizenship: How Migrant Suffering Sustains White Democracy

Hil Malatino
Trans Care

Sarah Juliet Lauro
Kill the Overseer! The Gamification of Slave Resistance

Alexis L. Boylan, Anna Mae Duane, Michael Gill, and Barbara Gurr
Furious Feminisms: Alternate Routes on *Mad Max: Fury Road*

Ian G. R. Shaw and Marv Waterstone
Wageless Life: A Manifesto for a Future beyond Capitalism

Claudia Milian
LatinX

Aaron Jaffe
Spoiler Alert: A Critical Guide

Don Ihde
Medical Technics

Jonathan Beecher Field
Town Hall Meetings and the Death of Deliberation

Jennifer Gabrys
How to Do Things with Sensors

Naa Oyo A. Kwate
Burgers in Blackface: Anti-Black Restaurants Then and Now

Arne De Boever
Against Aesthetic Exceptionalism

Steve Mentz
Break Up the Anthropocene

John Protevi
Edges of the State

Matthew J. Wolf-Meyer
Theory for the World to Come: Speculative Fiction and Apocalyptic Anthropology

Nicholas Tampio
Learning versus the Common Core

Kathryn Yusoff
A Billion Black Anthropocenes or None

Kenneth J. Saltman
The Swindle of Innovative Educational Finance

Ginger Nolan
The Neocolonialism of the Global Village

Joanna Zylinska
The End of Man: A Feminist Counterapocalypse

Robert Rosenberger
Callous Objects: Designs against the Homeless

William E. Connolly
Aspirational Fascism: The Struggle for Multifaceted Democracy under Trumpism

Chuck Rybak
UW Struggle: When a State Attacks Its University

(Continued on page 120)

Only a Black Athlete Can Save Us Now

Grant Farred

University of Minnesota Press

MINNEAPOLIS

LONDON

ISBN 978-1-5179-1337-3 (PB)
ISBN 978-1-4529-6716-5 (Ebook)
ISBN 978-1-4529-6742-4 (Manifold)

Published by the University of Minnesota Press
111 Third Avenue South, Suite 290
Minneapolis, MN 55401-2520
http://www.upress.umn.edu

Available as a Manifold edition at manifold.umn.edu

The University of Minnesota is an equal-opportunity educator and employer.

To Ian Balfour: Raptors partisan, Expos loyalist, music aficionado, and possessor of a truly capacious mind

Contents

Prologue   xi

1. The NBA and the WNBA Are the Most
   Progressive Forces in American Politics   1

2. From "Fear the Deer" to
   "Follow the Deer"   7

3. Out of One, Many   19

4. Reforming the Unreformable   25

5. *Nur ein Gott kann uns jetzt Retten*   35

6. Strange Things Happen in the Bubble   37

7. "Hey, Chicago, What Do You Say?"   41

8. The WNBA Takes Its Stance   43

9. Colin Kaepernick   51

10. Silence Reverberates   57

11. The Peculiar Science of Black
    Athletic Entropy   61

12. The Burden of Over-Representation,
    Curiously Borne by Woods and Jordan   71

13. Change Is Everywhere, or So It Seems   75

14. Change Is Everywhere, Even the NHL   81

15. Biting the Hand That Feeds Them   85

16. A Pause for a Cause   95

17. Ontological Exhaustion   99

18. Inverse Displacement   103

19. Love, Unrequited   109

20. From L.A. to Kenosha   115

21. Harmolodics   117

    Acknowledgments   119

Prologue

ONLY A BLACK ATHLETE CAN SAVE US NOW is an essay that should come with a warning label. One that reads "Misleading Title." Or, maybe, if one were generous, "Slightly Misleading Title." The dissembling assumes an even-more serious aspect because, as will be seen momentarily, this essay is addressed to my son, Ezra, himself an aspiring—soon-to-be teen—black athlete.

However, the ambivalence about the title derives from an obtrusive recognition. That is, this essay is as much an acknowledgement of the important role played by athletes, and black athletes in particular, during the Covid-19 pandemic and the racist violence that marked—and marred—2020, as it is an articulation of the limits of what these athletes can do. Indeed, in some of its more reflective moments, this essay offers a pointed critique of what it is that these athletes do. And, by extension, what it is that they fail to do—what they cannot do.

However, much as this essay is in a dialectical struggle with itself about the role of the black athlete in a moment of historic crisis, *Only a Black Athlete Can Save Us Now* undertakes this work toward a very specific end. On the one hand, this essay recognizes the importance of the athletes' reformist tendencies and objectives. Some of the athletes' undertaking are more urgent than others. In truth, some are even radical. Most prominent among these is the campaign to end police violence (a stand that constitutes arguably the key moment in this essay), a movement fundamental to simply keeping black Americans alive. The events of George Floyd (killed by a police officer's knee, Minneapolis, 2020), Lt. Caron Lazario (a uniformed U.S. Army officer pepper sprayed by a police officer, Virginia, 2021), Daunte Wright (Brooklyn Center, Minnesota, 2021, shot by a police officer, Kim Potter)[1] and Andrew Brown (Elizabeth City, North Carolina, April, 2021)[2] are but some of the most high profile instances that have led to the widespread call to defund the police.[3] A movement that achieved its first statutory success in April 2021, when the Maryland legislature voted to overturn the state's police Bill of Rights; the officers Bill of Rights protects the police from investigation and prosecution for acts committed in the execution of their duties, rights not afforded ordinary citizens. The Maryland state legislature also gave civilians greater oversight of the policing.[4] A historic enactment for a state still living with the aftermath of the 2015 death of Freddie Gray, a black man, at the hands of Baltimore police officers.

On the other hand, *Only A Black Athlete Can Save Us Now* is impatient with the reformist discourse as advocated by these athletes, impatient because this movement is so deeply attached to the political. This essay argues against representative politics, not only as it constitutes the entire horizon of possibility, but because representative politics has come to stand as a, or the, democratic end in itself. That is, "democracy" has come to mean—has long since

1. At the time of writing, April 2021, Potter is facing a second-degree murder charge.
2. https://www.msn.com/en-us/news/crime/andrew-brown-jrs-rela-tive-disputes-official-account-of-the-fatal-police-shooting/ar-BB1gdhJE?o-cid=uxbndlbing.
3. https://www.msn.com/en-us?refurl=%2fen-us%2fnews%2fus%2f1-verdict-then-6-police-killings-across-america-in-24-hours%2far-BB1g0sY-W%3focid%3dspartan-dhp-feeds.
4. https://www.msn.com/en-us/news/politics/maryland-becomes-first-state-to-repeal-police-bill-of-rights-overriding-hogan-veto/ar-BB1f-w7yc?ocid=uxbndlbing. The Democrat-controlled legislature overrode the veto of Republican governor Larry Hogan.

meant—securing the franchise, legally guaranteeing it and ensuring that it is freely practiced. "Democracy" so understood follows the logic that the state is in need of drastic overhaul, rather than working to ensure that the state will "wither away," as Marx hoped. All the while representative "democracy" maintains the system of late-capitalism, espousing the language of (securing) "opportunity for all" rather than organizing for the systematic dismantling of the state and late-capitalism so that a different future might be imagined. Politics, so conceived, constitutes the very ground of reformism in our moment.

To this end, Lenin's notion of dual power is pivotal to this essay's argument. *In* Only A Black Athlete Can Save Us Now, *dual power designates a simultaneous struggle on two fronts. The first takes place within the existing structures of power, named "reformism" here, while the second assigns to itself the work of thinking a much more radical—utopian—organization of society. As such, dual power refuses subreption. Dual power will not mistake the secondary, reformism, for the primary. It is the reorganization of society, wrenching it forever out of late-capitalism, that must, now more than ever, be prioritized. Subreption is that intellectual modality that reminds us not to mistake that which is itself part of the problem, in this case representative democracy, as a panacea. Instead, representative democracy must be properly apprehended. That is, securing the universal franchise is but the temporary means of struggle—much as it enables us to rally against racism, xenophobia, economic inequality and so on. However, in the end reformism itself must be undone. Reformism, then, as the autoimmune means of achieving utopia. Reformism as a political mechanism intended to render itself not only anachronistic, but ultimately subject to superannuation.*

In place of Lenin's soviets and the (rapidly declining) Czarist state, *Only a Black Athlete Can Save Us Now* conceives of distinct roles for (athlete-driven) reformism and an impulse toward a utopianism much indebted to Fredric Jameson's thought-provoking essay "An American Utopia." Jameson's thinking is augmented by the spirit of that singular band of mid-nineteenth-century American communists. Also known as Associationists, these communist utopian groups included "Mother Lee's" Shakers, Robert Owen's New Harmony project, Charles Fourier's phalanxes (of which the most famous is the Brook Farm collective, in which Horace Greeley, Margaret Fuller and Ralph Waldo Emerson participated), Étienne Cabet's Icarians, and John Humphrey Noyes's Oneida Perfectionists.[5] Living in an antebellum America on the brink of the Civil War and in a society existentially at war with itself, these Associationists were, each in their own way, idealists determined to break with the world as it was. Seeking a different mode of being in the world, they sought to enact a rupture between themselves and their society. These Associationists were, inter alia, practitioners of free love, women's liberation, and equality and complex marriage; many of them were back-to-the-land Romantics (they almost all failed in their attempts to work the land, in large measure because they lacked the skills necessary to run a farming enterprise). Most of them were proponents of communes in which private property was forsworn. In their ranks were also eugenicists, millennial Christians, agnostics, and atheists. Many were anticapitalist, but there was also one successful entrepreneurial venture—this singular honorific belongs to Noyes's Oneida community.[6] These communists sought to build a world in which they could give full expression to their "free will." A world over which the state and its representative apparatuses had no hold.

That world in which Fourier's *The Theory of the Four Movements,* Owen's *A New View of Society,* and Cabet's *Voyage en Icarie* (a work that echoes the founding utopian text, Thomas More's *Utopia*) found its audience and, for a brief moment, flourished, was, like ours, a

5. See Chris Jennings's *Paradise Now: The Story American Utopianism* (New York: Random House, 2016) for an overview of these movements.

6. See, in this regard, Ellen Wayland-Smith's *Oneida: From Free Love Utopia to the Well-Set Table* (New York: Picador, 2016). Wayland-Smith is a descendant of one of the original Community families. Hers is an especially keen critique of both the Perfectionists' capacity to generate capital and sustain economic growth and the oddly communitarian notion of that undertaking.

dystopic moment. Indeed, ours may be more so. Everywhere, in 2020, it appeared that there was chaos. Wherever we turned, there was hopelessness and despair. In the midst of this there was, however, moments of selflessness, concern for the other, and courage too. Largely, however, 2020 revealed lives overwrought by existential precarity, a conjuncture defined by a racism on the rise in the United States and a Covid-19 pandemic that laid bare a late-capitalism in all its ruthlessness.

Saliently, however, we encountered a late-capitalism cutting a wider swathe. It wreaked havoc on, as crises always do, the most economically vulnerable—the working poor, the indigent, the desperate "illegal" immigrants; the pandemic also represented a special threat to the incarcerated, who found themselves entirely at the mercy of the state. More than that, however, our conjuncture witnessed the rise of a late-capitalism that also has those in the American middle class in its sights. The historically poor, people of color, impoverished rural communities, found themselves joined in line at food banks by those who had just yesterday imagined themselves as immune to the predations of capital. Long, snaking lines of cars, stretching for miles across the length and breadth of the country. Understanding themselves to be economically secure and medically safe just a moment ago, that always expansive constituency known as the American middle class took their place alongside those who have long known financial want and material scarcity. Large numbers of Americans with distinct socioeconomic statuses, all of them waiting for a box containing the most alimentary of goods: canned food, bottled water, toilet paper.

Not quite Steinbeck's Joad family, not quite. But then again, this storm, while dust-free, is showing itself to be a very different animal. Maybe even an all-consuming one. A creature that may or may not be brought to heel by a series of federal works programs. Ours is an economic and a public health crisis, set against the backdrop of what is surely, lest we act swiftly, a looming—looming ever larger—environmental disaster. Ours is a time tailor-made for utopian thinking.

The *longue durée* that is 2020 is an economic crisis that increasingly seems to resemble the Great Depression of the last century rather than the Great Recession of 2008. And the racism, in its blatancy, at least, would seem to belong to that of an earlier vintage. Racism is energized now, given impetus, no matter that he has been electorally defeated, by a former American president who has a long history of racism. In fact, he has a family history of racism, dating back to his father, Fred Trump, a fascist fellow-traveler, Klan sympathizer, no matter that such unsightly affiliations are now largely ignored.

Arrayed against this onslaught against minority life are athletes, in a variety of sports. At the forefront of this movement, in the most complicated way possible, are players in the National Basketball Association (NBA) and their women's equivalent, the WNBA. Professional basketballers have placed themselves in the vanguard of the struggle against police brutality against black bodies. Most of the players engaged in this struggle, but by no means all of them, are black. They are, all of them, trying to forge a way forward, determined to produce some structural reform in our deeply unequal world; at least some, especially as it pertains to voting and broader minority participation in the U.S. electoral process; intent on protecting the black, Latino and Asian American vote against latter-day Jim Crow legislation as enacted in Georgia in 2021 after the Republicans suffered losses there in the 2020 presidential elections and in the 2021 Senate races.

Most importantly, the protesting athletes are not limited to America. Footballers across the world (as distinct from their grid-iron American cousins), as well as cricketers and rugby players, among many others, too made their voices heard. In this spirit, the signal non-American athlete in *Only a Black Athlete Can Save Us Now* is a black Briton, Lewis Hamilton, the reigning—and seven-time—Formula I (FI) champion. Hamilton is unarguably the non-American who has done most to champion the cause of black life in America internationally, bringing attention not only to the killing of

George Floyd in May 2020, but highlighting the cause of Breonna Taylor, a black woman shot to death in her own home in Louisville, Kentucky. Broadly speaking, Hamilton has dedicated himself to shining the world's spotlight on the vulnerability of black life to police violence in America.

However, Hamilton, a vegan and a man much beloved of the American popular, is central to *Only a Black Athlete Can Save Us Now* not only because of his determined antiracist stance. He is critical to this essay because of his commitment to issues such as global warming. Our stewardship of the planet has led Hamilton to be critical of the ways in which the FI "circus," which covers hundreds of thousands of miles in the cause of its season, from Brazil to Bahrain, from Montreal to Monaco, is responsible for environmental degradation. Hamilton has also been outspoken in the cause of human rights. Although, in truth, if human rights were seriously engaged as an issue, Hamilton would have his work cut out for him. He would have to take aim at not only the usual suspects—those countries that routinely abuse its own citizens. Bahrain, Turkey, China and Russia are obvious but, of course, justifiable, targets. He would also have to account for the United States, Brazil, Hungary and Singapore. In fact, by any strict definition of the abuse of human rights, there is hardly a country on the F1 schedule that would be exempt from criticism.

Bearing this in mind, Hamilton has been an outspoken advocate of planetary responsibility. To this end, Hamilton has long since banned the use of all plastic in his office. In so doing, he may be the athlete to nudge our thinking in the direction of, if not the utopian (although I see no reason to suppress that impulse), then at least a more "wholistic" course of action to reimagining our world.

It is not, then, a matter of pitting Hamilton against, say, a figure such as LeBron James, because each in their own way offers valid critiques of the conditions under which black lives are lived. After all, James's More Than a Vote advocacy group, an organization founded by athletes to combat voter suppression, played a key role in mobilizing minority voters in the 2020 election.[7] After all, in the wake of winning his 7th FI championship, Hamilton clearly stated that, as the only black driver in the history of his sport, he was more motivated to win in 2020 precisely because of his opposition to racism. In short, he identified the Black Lives Matter movement as the raison d'etre of his 2020 triumph. And so, rather than a dialectical framing, this essay presents Hamilton as that athlete who can help us think beyond a single issue—as important as, say, racism is—in order to propose ways in which racism, the threat of environmental devastation, and growing economic inequality brought about by the ravages of late-capitalism be taken up together—that is, as equally important issues, issues bound together in a nonhierarchical relationship. Issues interlinked, issues that demand simultaneous address. What emerges out of this need for an expanded engagement with the perils that threaten planetary survival is the imperative to combine LeBron and Hamilton's projects. To combine LeBron's struggle to keep black bodies alive with Hamilton's injunction that we think how it is we are in the world; that we undertake the work of articulating how it is we want to live.

The Bubble: A Brief Utopian Excursus

As both the NBA and the National Hockey League (NHL) showed in the organization of their 2020 postseasons, a certain communitarian thinking was already underway. Because of the pandemic, the NBA (in Florida) and the NHL (in Toronto and Edmonton)[8] created bubbles so that they could create conditions that would, under the conditions of a pandemic, ensure the health and safety of their players, coaches, support staff, referees, and the venues' myriad employees. As NBA commissioner Adam Silver explains, the bubble was designed to be

7. https://www.morethanavote.org/. NBA players were especially prominent in this organization.

8. https://lasvegassun.com/news/2020/jul/26/life-inside-the-nhl-bubble-vgk-arrive-edmonton-pla/.

its own self-supporting world, but not one that was entirely removed from the surrounding community. As such, Silver understood, the bubble was no absolute guarantee against the raging pandemic. In thoughtful terms, Silver delineates a logic of mutual dependency and, saliently, the shared vulnerability of all who constituted bubble life:

> When we first began proposing playing in a bubble-type environment, I had many individual calls with players who were nervous, understandably, as to how safe it that would even be. . . . Part of it was the sense that the players were going to be dependent on the behavior of everyone else in the bubble community: players, staff, employees—anyone who was a part of it. And they realized we were only going to be as safe as the least compliant participant.[9]

The NBA and NHL bubbles were a world removed from the athletes' ordinary lives. Cocooned in order to make it possible for them to play, they were at once competing against each other on the court (or, on the ice, as the case might be), responsible for each other's health (their mutual physical and well as mental well-being) and utterly exposed to each other. The players understood, were made to understand, that they were "only as safe as the least compliant participant." In terms of a worst-case scenario, the bubble was only as safe as the most irresponsible player; as such, the irresponsible self constituted a threat to all other selves. Alternately, in the best-case scenario, the "least compliant participant" is not one but all selves. That is, the "least compliant" bubble occupant is indistinguishable from the most "compliant" and so all are, for the sake of the affirmative argument, equally safe. In such an event, all selves can then be said to be working in the best interest of the other, and that of the self. Either way, everything depends upon the "least compliant" self's responsibility to itself and the other(s). As we have known, at least since Thomas More's *Utopia* and maybe even before that, since

9. "MOTY," *GQ*, December 2020 /January 2021, 112. (This is part of an interview Silver did with the journalist Bomani Jones.)

Plato's Republic, the dependence of each upon each determines the success or failure of all utopian projects.

As such, utopia opens us up to, in Emmanuel Levinas's terms, the possibility of "genuine experience" because it "transports us beyond what constitutes our nature. Genuine experience must even lead us beyond the nature that surrounds us, which is not jealous for the marvelous secrets it harbors, and, in complicity with men, submits to their reasons and inventions; in it men feel themselves to be at home."[10] The bubble as a "home" "beyond what constituted," before the pandemic, that place where professional athletes used to dwell, if not necessarily in Heidegger's sense of the term. The bubble presents a new way of being in relation to the other, a mode of being that goes well beyond what NBA and NHL players understood to be their "natural" habitat. Before the pandemic, NBA players—like all professional athletes—were free to do as they pleased in their off-time. Free to live "beyond" their teammates—that is, there was no compelling reason to be either constantly (physically) with or in constant contact with their teammates. The bubble changed that. Not only did teammates live cheek by jowl with each other in the same hotels, they did so with players from the other teams in the bubble. They ate together, rode the bus together to practices and games with players from other teams, socialized together—at the bar, poolside, as a temporarily nonpartisan collective. Self and other, as it were, made to live in frequent—daily— contact. A strangle social dynamic surely obtained. Opponents on the court, friends off of it. As free to socialize with their own teammates as they were to hang out with friends from an opposing team.

Secured against the world in their utopian enclaves, NBA players were nevertheless conflicted about how their profession—their standing as black men in America—insulated them momentarily against the predations of the pandemic, to say nothing of how it shielded them from America's racist violence.

---

10. Emmanuel Levinas, "Philosophy and the Idea of Infinity," in *Collected Philosophical Papers,* ed. Alphonso Lingis, 47–59 (Pittsburgh: Duquesne University Press, 1998), 47.

Uniquely in tune with their fellow-professionals, out of joint with the lived reality of their community. The NBA bubble as the space in which insularity, an entirely new register of sociopolitical reflection, intense self-critique, and personal uncertainty coexisted. Out of the NBA (and the NHL) bubble, utopia emerges not as the retreat from critique but rather as the most acute version, its material privileges notwithstanding, of what it means to live in association, as the Owenites might have insisted. It is a difficult thing, to learn to live together in an entirely new way.

The bubble as that place where personal and collective generosity can thrive. Russell Westbrook, then of the Oklahoma Thunder, now of the Washington Wizards,[11] reportedly left an $8,000 tip for the hotel staff when his team was knocked out of the playoffs. The bubble as that mode of encounter where individual differences are ratcheted up a notch or three because of living in unprecedented proximity to the other. (A joy for the self, a psychological strain on the self.)

The joys and the difficulties obtain, regardless of whether the other is a teammate, an opponent, a referee, or a coach. How to be in relation to the other is an ongoing struggle, no matter how luxurious or reduced the material conditions. And yet, returned to civilian life, the Boston Celtics guard Jayson Tatum found himself at a loss as to how live outside the bubble: "'Damn, do I miss the bubble?'"[12]

The bubble, in Tatum's recollection, as less a rude rupture with what-is and what-has-been and more a revelation of what Levinas conceives as the "marvelous secret" of a "genuine experience"; or, the bubble as the gateway to utopia.[13] The bubble as a space of duty—

---

11. As of July 2021, Westbrook became a member of the L.A. Lakers.

12. Taylor Rooks, "The Most Magical Place on Earth: Inside the NBA Bubble Experiment," *GQ*, November 2020, 119.

13. In his essay "The Dwelling," Levinas offers another opening into how a secure space might allow for the possibility of utopia: "The access to the world is produced in a movement that starts from the utopia of the dwelling and traverses a space to effect a primordial grasp, to seize and to take away. The uncertain future of the element is suspended . . . This grasp operated on the elemental is labor" (Levinas, "The Dwelling," in

*when autonomy supersedes heteronomy, per Kant's distinction where
individual responsibility takes precedence over individual desire—that
is also a space in which historical moments are in conflict with each
other. The bubble (or "heterotopia," to bastardize Michel Foucault's
concept) as that space in which what-is finds itself exposed to the
prospect of its own eradication or replacement with what-might-be.
That is, where Kantian individual responsibility melds with—or mutates into—collective desire.*

Hamilton's position is not to suggest that environmental racism and critiques of a vampiric capitalism is a new phenomenon.
Anything but. A veritable body of literature on the subject exists,
a literature that can be said to have first announced itself in 1492.
However, in our world, where capitalism is "more than just an economic system: it is an existential conflict felt deep in our bones, our
minds, and our ecosystems. For centuries the great war of enclosure
has privatized soils, seas, and airs—dispossessing billions of their
lands, livelihoods, and dignity,"[14] carpe diem is, in several moments
if not in its entirety, the governing logic of *Only a Black Athlete Can
Save Us Now*.

Capitalism has "dispossessed billions of their lands and their
livelihoods." Capitalism is the pandemic, Corona is the virus; capitalism is the disease, Corona is merely the most recent symptom.
In conjunction with racism, capitalism has put paid to millions of
lives and stripped billions of their "dignity." The Fourierists and the
Perfectionists set themselves against the dystopia that was indus-
trial capitalism. All the while, of course, they did little if anything
to oppose slavery. Indeed, the Perfectionists undertook a eugenicist
experiment (which led to the reproduction of the "stirpicults"—
the offspring of select breeding between the best and the brightest

---

Totality and Infinity: An Essay on Exteriority, trans. Alphonso Lingis, 152–62
[Pittsburgh: Duquesne University Press, 2005], 158).

14. Ian G. R. Shaw and Marv Whitestone, *Wageless Life: A Manifesto
for a Life beyond Capitalism* (Minneapolis: University of Minnesota Press,
2019), 1.

of the Perfectionists), even as they employed black and working-class white labor to perform menial tasks in their Oneida, New York, Mansion House; they also hired local hands—that is, non-community members—first in their trap-making and later in their cutlery businesses. Oneida, like the other nineteenth-century utopians, reserved utopia for the white few.

Crisis Is Opportunity

Notwithstanding, it might be worth turning once more to that hoary old chestnut that crisis is opportunity. In this im-perfect storm of racism, environmental degradation, rapacious capitalism, and a global pandemic, in the midst of an unprecedented existential crisis, let us reconceive Lenin's guiding question. At stake is not what is to be done. The answer to that is plain, self-evident, if seemingly insurmountable. Put an end to capitalism, do whatever is necessary to heal the planet, outlaw all forms of discrimination, and, last but by no means least, find a new, sustainable mode of democratic life. A life free, as Jameson urges us, of the overbearing apparatuses of representation.

If crisis is indeed opportunity, then the multiple, mutually rein-forcing (to devastating effect, no less) vectors that constitute our crisis must be taken not as an impossibility. Instead, so substantial and life-threatening is the crisis that we need not be held hostage by it. Rather, we are freed by the crisis to reconstruct our world. In its entirety. From top to bottom. Our moment has made of Lenin's injunction a question fit for the age. A question that is really an imperative. How could we not do what needs to be done?

After all, the Covid-19 pandemic, the on-going murderous assault on black life, the brutal effects of economic inequality, and the obvious biopolitical costs of environmental degradation has made abundantly clear to us the extent of our crisis. If we do not take up, so to speak, the utopian cudgels now, then we will have failed our moment. We will have failed ourselves. If the effect of the pandemic is to, say, for a brief but memorable moment, make the Himalayas visible to the residents of New Delhi because of the drastic reduction in pollution, then surely we can glimpse or dream of other such vistas? What else is possible?

No Return to Normal

At the very least, we should commit to this: there will be no return to normal. For the other, normal was George Floyd, Breonna Taylor, Daunte Wright. Normal was denial of access to adequate healthcare, a condition that the pandemic has revealed in all its ugliness. (And when I say "was," I really mean "is" as the present-future, as what obtains and is likely to persist.) In Western nations such as the United States, supply exceeds demand, while not a single dose is available in Haiti; Israel boasts of its high vaccination rate while Palestinians in the Occupied Territories are left scrambling to secure what they can. The poorest nations on earth are left to fend for themselves. Normal was eternal economic precarity, the everyday reality of those deemed disposable populations, populations growing ever-more populous in number, stretched across the globe. For the other, normal was systemic exclusion from affordable housing, normal was subjecting the other to an education unworthy of its name. For the other normal was, in short, an alimentary struggle, not the least of which was to secure sufficient food. It is the other who knows "food scarcity" and "food insecurity," it is the other who is intimate with the lack of access to clean water. At all costs, we must resist a return to normal. The slogan No Return to Normal stands as the refusal to reinstate the brutalities of inequality.

If crisis is indeed opportunity, then it is underwritten by a historic charge. We are called upon to imagine a new way of being in the world. That is, we must set about building, in concrete terms, new structures that determine our relationship to each other. Of all the nineteenth-century utopians, the Perfectionist experiment survived longer than any other—for some four decades, from around 1840 to 1880. What is more, for a long period, unlike their peers, they thrived. First by building traps, then by manufacturing plated silver. Even when the Oneida Association dissolved, Oneida Community Limited continued, until it fell into bankruptcy in 2006. All the while it retained many traces of its founder John Humphrey Noyes's utopian vision. Apart, that is, from Noyes sexual mores, which the "stirpicults," several of whom Noyes himself had fathered, and their descendants eschewed in favor of bourgeois respectability. (The "stirpicults" returned determinedly to the nuclear family, no matter that many of these alliances resulted in the intermarriage of the offspring of the most prominent Oneida families.)

The Mansion House, the Perfectionist abode, remains standing, as I can attest after Ezra and I made a visit there in December 2020. A testament to the materiality of utopianism. In the Mansion House dwells, in varying degrees, the spirit of Fourier's phalanxes, Owens's "New Harmony" and Cabet's planned Icarian villages. A materiality secured, in Levinas's phrasing, because of work: "This grasp operated on the elemental is labor."[15]

If we cannot, in a moment of such intense global vulnerability, unequal in the extreme, as I have noted, take up the cudgels now, then when? Is now not the moment take up the apocalyptic challenge thrown down by Slavoj Žižek in that most memorable rendering of our late-capitalist quandary: "It is easier to imagine the end of the world than the end of capitalism"? After all, utopianism asks us to think about being the world in a completely different way. The athletes have taken the lead. It remains now for utopian thinking to undo the damages done to those untold billions. If not now, when? If not through dual power, then how will we make our world anew? If we can recognize simultaneously what it is the athletes have made possible and what it is they cannot do, then the warning label that announces this essay will not have been in vain.

On second—or, third, as the case might be—thoughts, everything may hinge on us recognizing that any possibility for a livable

15. Levinas, "Dwelling," 158.

future—that is, sustainable, beginning with the environment—will require a more trenchant statement. It is only the end of capitalism that can save us. Our Levinasian "work" is to build a world, our world, without capitalism.

1. The NBA and the WNBA Are the Most Progressive Forces in American Politics

Nur ein Gott kann uns jetzt retten.
—MARTIN HEIDEGGER, *Der Spiegel*

Thank God for my brothers in the NBA.
—CORNEL WEST *to Anderson Cooper, August 27, 2020*

TODAY, MY SON, EVERYTHING CHANGES. Today, August 27th, 2020, everything changes. It changes because a black man walked into an NBA locker room. He had his mind made up. He had decided that he would not do something. He would not do the very thing he was expected to do, something he was paid to do. The thing that everyone in the locker room was about to do. He would not play basketball.

I cannot recall how many times I have said to myself that everything is going to change. Too often in the past I have been disappointed by my own prognostications, swept along, wrongly, on a tide called "optimism." (And not, I admit, optimism of the Gramscian variety—"pessimism of the intellect, optimism of the will." The result, maybe, of too much Antonio Gramsci and not enough of Friedrich Nietzsche's Zarathustra.) I have subscribed to the belief, misbegotten or not, that tomorrow will, inevitably, through the inexorable force that is history, be better; tomorrow will be markedly different for black life in America than it was yesterday. Nonetheless, today I find myself—once more, as I have for most of my life—marveling, I use the word reluctantly, but I marvel at the power of sport. Once more I stand moved, touched, amazed at the power of athletes to commit themselves to changing our world.

So, while I do my best to eschew optimism, it is my duty to record, as a lifelong student and fan of sport, how professional black athletes, in the spirit of James Baldwin's imploring black Americans to take responsibility for their white counterparts, are making their voices heard. How professional black athletes are trying to save black lives from brutal white American violence. I do not know what the effects of the athletes' actions will be. I expect that it will be, as these things are, complicated. Uneven. A sprig of hope here, a dollop or three of disappointment there. I am trying to understand, maybe even to anticipate, how this all turns out. If it sounds, then, as though I am vacillating, then it is not because I am hedging my bets, as a good Gramscian might do—you know, "optimism of the will," that kind of thing—but because I am doing my best to sift through the possibilities. In preparation, and one can never be fully prepared, for what might eventuate, preparation foreshadowed by possibility and uncertainty, finding myself equally in the throes of profound foreboding and the sense that now, as is surely clear to you, is the moment to go all in on utopia.

I write to you Ezra in no small measure because your mother and I are watching your love for basketball grow. We watched your first game, in the fall of 2019, without expectation, just happy to see you take up a team sport. But you, you had other plans. You blossomed. You went from playing for your proudly uncompetitive school team—so entrenched in the feel-good culture of crunchy-granola Ithaca—to being recruited to the Wolf Pack, the best team in our immediate area; after which you were asked to join another (travel) team, the Binghamton Bulldogs. In Ithaca, the Wolf Pack is the most elite team, and your coach, R., who combines keen instruction with his deep, smiling, love for the game, is outstanding. The difference, my son, between a good coach and an exceptional one is, it turns out, rather simple. A good coach helps you become the best player you imagine yourself capable of becoming. An exceptional coach presents you with a vision of yourself beyond your own imagining. R. is undoubtedly an exceptional coach. He saw from the very time he watched you play (way back in 2019), and continues to see, potential in you that he draws out, that he nurtures into being.

Your mother and I delight in how you have taken to the game. It is quite something to see how you are making it central to your sense of who you are. It is out your love for the game and our love for you that I am writing you.

Nip (my nickname for Ezra), you look up to the likes of Anthony Davis and LeBron James of the Los Angeles Lakers, you idolize Joel Embiid and Ben Simmons of the Philadelphia 76ers. On the Wolf Pack you wear number 25, in honor of the black Australian American Simmons. You make fun of James Harden's defense—a deficiency fed, with good reason, by YouTube videos in which Harden plays defense like a matador. Walt Clyde Frazier, the greatest Knick of all and the Knicks color commentator, calls this "matador D."[1] (But, I promise, James Harden has a defensive surprise for you.) Nonetheless, you look covetously at Harden's three-point shooting ability. You mock, with good reason, my beloved, the perennially hapless New York Knicks, even though you've taken a shine to Julius Randle. (I wish you'd seen Patrick Ewing in his pomp, my son. Oh, how I wish. Much as I wish I'd seen Walt Clyde in his prime.) In taking their stand against racism, taking especial aim at police brutality against black men and women, these NBA and WNBA players showed themselves to be the most progressive force in American politics. Progressive in the sense that they have pinpointed exactly what it is that ails American society and in demanding that these issues be redressed. Progressive in the sense that they understand police brutality as Martin Luther King

---

1. The term "matador D" is Walt Clyde Frazier's, the former New York Knick guard and the team's longtime color commentator. I first heard Frazier, the greatest Knick of all, use the phrase in the 1990s in relation to the former Knicks guard Mark Jackson. According to Frazier, Jackson played "matador D": "He just waved opponents by."

4 ONLY A BLACK ATHLETE CAN SAVE US NOW
Jr. does in his denunciation of the bombing of black churches in Mississippi: "This is white power in its most brutal, cold-blooded and vicious form."[2] Amen. Or, goddamn, as the case might be.

These NBA and WNBA players are bringing attention to racism, violence against women, educational inequity, voter suppression,[3] the lack of economic prospect for minority communities, and police brutality. These athletes are taking it upon themselves to do whatever it is they can to ensure social justice for the black community. In doing so, these black athletes are undertaking to create life—black life, yes, but also life in this country in its entirety—that can withstand, and possibly overcome, the hatred that spews from a significant constituency of white America; a constituency that can only be named white supremacist. A hatred aimed squarely at black America. These black athletes have embarked upon an onerous undertaking, my son, but, as Baldwin knows, this is the kind of work that black America is so often asked to do. There is always salvific work to be done. By black America. As it is today, as was yesterday, and as it will surely be tomorrow.

Baldwin knows this. In "My Dungeon Shook," his letter to his nephew and namesake, James, Baldwin implores his nephew to do this work,[4] all the while seeking to fortify young James with the strength of their forbears in this epic undertaking:

2. Martin Luther King, Jr., *Where Do We Go from Here: Chaos or Community?* (Boston: Beacon Press, 2010), 34.

3. In the wake of the 2020 election, states such as Georgia and Michigan are enacting restrictive voting laws designed to suppress minority turnout because these constituencies proved critical to Republican losses in that cycle. Following the enacting of this legislation, Major League Baseball moved the 2021 All Star game from Atlanta to Denver. Corporate America, behemoth Coca Cola is headquartered in Atlanta, added its voice to the protest, prompting Republican Senate Minority Leader Mitch McConnell to, irony of ironies, warn big business to "stay out of politics." Of course, what McConnell really meant was, "Keep blacks out of politics."

4. An injunction that should come with a Nietzschean warning: "Dangerous is it to be an heir." Friedrich Nietzsche, *Zarathustra,* trans. Thomas Common (New York: Modern Library, 1909), 81.

We can make America what America must become. It will be hard, James, but you come from sturdy, peasant stock, men who picked cotton and dammed rivers and built railroads, and, in the teeth of the most terrifying odds, achieved an unassailable and monumental dignity.[5]

To "make America what it must become," the work begins where it always does:[6] with trying to stop white America killing black Americans. You see, my son, when it mattered, when one more black person had been shot by a white police officer ("white power in its most brutal, cold-blooded and vicious form"), players in the NBA and the WNBA took their place in the vanguard of a political struggle. What is more, they did so with a political thoroughness that cannot be gainsaid. Nor did it not hurt that these athletes also have a certain flair for the dramatic. Both when it comes to their on-court theatrics and in their response to racism in America.

5. James Baldwin, *The Fire Next Time* (New York: Dial Press, 1963), 24.

6. I take up Baldwin, King, and issues around sport in *An Essay for Ezra: Racial Terror in America* (Minneapolis: University of Minnesota Press, 2021), a work that is in many ways a dialectical companion piece to this essay.

2. From "Fear the Deer" to "Follow the Deer"

THE NBA PLAYERS were led by the Milwaukee Bucks. The Bucks' slogan, part catchy, part Midwest feelgood, is "Fear the Deer." (Deer are a dangerous hazard, anywhere in the country, on a deserted road late at night, but hardly a fearsome creature.) On August 26, however, they acted not because they wanted their NBA (immediate) opponents, the Orlando Magic, to "fear" the Milwaukee "Deer." Rather, the Bucks acted in such a way as to make evident—audible, if you wish—the deep existential fear that all black Americans experience as a daily occurrence, as a matter of routine. It does not matter whether a black person is on the street, as in the case of George Floyd in Minneapolis (May 2020) or Daunte Wright (Brooklyn Center, April 2021), or is, as the vernacular expression goes (an idiomatic expression possessed of its own hard truth), driving while black—DWB. For a black person to be stopped by a white cop is both routine and never a routine matter for black people in this country. It is routine in that it happens all-too frequently. In truth, to DWB we should add ambulatory while black. For a black person, just making a quick grocery store stop, as happened to the Milwaukee Bucks' Sterling Brown, can lead to you being stun-gunned even as your actions present no threat to the police.[1]

1. https://www.tmj4.com/news/local-news/milwaukee-bucks-player-sterling-brown-sues-milwaukee-over-stun-gun-arrest. In truth, Brown was

Being alive while black. There are moments when such a declaration seems anything but hyperbole.

The upshot of all this is to instill dread in all black people. It is, as many black parents would readily testify, the fear that keeps them awake at night and haunts their every waking hour.

I know that you share this fear Ezra because I felt you tense up during the police scenes when we watched The Hate U Give *at our local cineplex.*

Worrying about what the outcome of a routine traffic stop might be. And black Americans are concerned not only for their teenage son or daughter or son. They are equally worried about what might happen when the police stop their aging father or their middle-aged, law-abiding sister.

On Wednesday, August 26th, 2020, the Bucks were scheduled to play the Magic at 4 p.m. in the NBA bubble, an athletic campus at ESPN's Wide World of Sports arena in Orlando, Florida. (Chosen, as we know, so as to protect the players, coaches, and their support staff, as well as the various workers whose responsibility it was to house and feed the players, while also keeping the facility sanitized—that is, free of the virus.) All the NBA playoff teams were accommodated in, and restricted to, the bubble to ensure that they could play safely during the Covid-19 pandemic.

Bursting the "Bubble"

The Bucks were scheduled to play the hometown team, the Orlando Magic—not that "hometown" had any meaning since all the games were played in arenas emptied of everyone except those personnel essential to the bubble. (Only in the later rounds did some families join the players in the bubble.) Following the usual pregame rou-

---

parked—illegally—across a handicapped space, but it was the early morning hours and less than three minutes passed between his exiting his car and returning to it. About this there can be no doubt: if Sterling Brown were a white man, he would not have endured such a fate.

tine, the Magic were out on court, going through their regulation warmups. If any of the Magic players did glance over to the other side of the court, none of them registered any surprise. Why they did not is itself surprising. Because, lo and behold, the other side of the court was empty. Initially, some—by which I mean TV commentators, post ipso facto, as well as a range other talking heads from the world of sport—thought that there were Bucks players who had succumbed to the Covid-19 virus. A reasonable conclusion, considering that the pandemic had cut a swathe through America, averaging one thousand deaths a day during the summer of 2020.

Whatever the speculation, there were no "Deer" to "Fear." The "Deer," it turned out, were engaged in the work of addressing black fear in their home state, Wisconsin. Turns out that it all began with a single "Deer."

Meet George Hill

The Bucks were led by George Hill.[2] An African American backup guard, Hill is a thirteen-year veteran of the NBA. His time in the NBA includes stints with the San Antonio Spurs (who drafted him with their first-round pick in 2008) and the Indiana Pacers (he was traded to his hometown Pacers in exchange for Kawhi Leonard, one of my favorite players). Thereafter, Hill briefly donned the uniforms of the Utah Jazz, the Sacramento Kings and the Cleveland Cavaliers (where he played with LeBron James) before arriving in Milwaukee.[3] Hill had decided, before entering the locker room on August 26, that he was not going to play. He had not told his team-

---

2. In August 2021, Hill rejoined the Bucks from the Philadelphia 76ers, to whom he had been traded midseason from the Oklahoma Thunder. Hill, I regret to say, will join the 2020–21 NBA champion Bucks without having been a member of their championship-winning team.

3. At the end of the 2019–2020 season, Hill was traded to the Oklahoma Thunder, and in 2021 he was traded again, this time to the Philadelphia 76ers.

mates about his decision prior to entering the locker room. Hill had only informed the Bucks' coach, Mike Budenholzer.[4]

Hill withheld his decision from his teammates in part because he did not want them to be burdened with the effects of his decision. After all, the Bucks were in the middle of a playoff series. Hill's mind, however, was made up. He would not dress. George Hill, as I said, is a backup guard. He is not the Bucks' star player. At a towering 6'11, that honor belongs to the Buck's MVP (and 2020 Defensive Player of the Year), Giannis Antetokounmpo. Popularly referred to as the "Greek Freak" for his otherworldly athleticism, Antetokounmpo, the Greek-born son of Nigerian parents, has such remarkable ball-handling skills for a big man that it is often he—rather than the guard, as is customary—who brings the ball up the floor for the Bucks. Of course, with his imposing size, Antetokounmpo is, it goes without saying, also a formidable presence around the rim, at both ends of the court. Hence that Defensive Player of the Year award and his two MVPs (Most Valuable Player awards—2018/19 and 2019/20).

Neither is Hill the second-best player on the Bucks. That honor belongs to the Khris Middleton, who plays a hybrid guard-forward position and is an efficient shooter. It is Middleton who is responsible for directing the Bucks plays when Antetokounmpo—often simply referred to as "Giannis"—is not heading the charge. The political role that Hill came to assume on the Bucks is incommensurate with—disproportionate to—his status on the Bucks roster. George Hill is no Muhammad Ali circa 1967, the dominant athlete in his profession taking a radical political stand against induction into the U.S. Army. George Hill is not John Carlos or Tommie Smith, raising a gloved fist on the podium at the 1968 Olympics. George Hill is not Serena Williams, a champion many times over and a tennis star not afraid of castigating racists. George Hill is not Naomi Osaka, the Haitian-Japanese (American-raised, trained and based) tennis player who used her triumphant run at the 2020 US Open to draw attention to victims of police brutality.

4. https://sports.yahoo.com/george-hill-planned-sit-solo-224801326.html?ocid=uxbndlbing.

On the road to winning her second U.S. Open title, from inside the professional tennis bubble, Osaka commemorated victims such as Breonna Taylor, Elijah McClain, and Tamir Rice, among others, by imprinting their names on her face mask.[5] Pandemic publicity at work, for all the world to see. Or, the kind of publicity only a pandemic can buy. George Hill is not LeBron James, who is not only among the best basketball players in the history of the game but the star to whom all others in the NBA, and in worlds well beyond it, look to for leadership in moments of crisis.

It is George Hill, however, for whom the realities of the moment—outside the bubble—were too pressing to be left unaddressed. To rephrase Rudiger Safranski's quasi-Newtonian terms, "Something was pressing in, so something had to press out."[6] Or, more to the point, something was pressing to get out because it no longer wished to be contained within. With good reason.

On Sunday, August 23, 2020, a white police officer, Rusten Sheskey, shot a black man, Jacob Blake, at least 7 times, in the back, in Kenosha, Wisconsin.[7] Kenosha is a mere forty miles southeast of Milwaukee. Jacob Blake survived, but his family has told the world that he will be paralyzed from the waist down for the rest of his life. Sheskey's bullets shattered Blake's spinal cord and his splintered his vertebrae, to say nothing of the damage done to his internal organs—surgeons had to remove almost his entire colon and his small intestine.

5. https://www.usatoday.com/story/sports/tennis/open/2020/09/12/naomi-osaka-racial-justice-masks-espn-us-open/5782139002/#:~:text-t=Naomi%20Osaka%2C%20who%20wore%20masks%20bearing%20the%20name,the%20point%20is%20to%20make%20people%20start%20talking.%22.

6. Rudiger Safranski, *Beyond Good and Evil,* trans. Ewald Osers (Cambridge, Mass.: Harvard University Press), 1999,

7. In April, 2021, Sheskey was cleared of any wrongdoing and returned to his position, having been on administrative leave after he shot Blake. https://chicago.cbslocal.com/2021/04/13/kenosha-police-officer-rusten-sheskey-returns-from-leave-jacob-blake-shooting/.

Hill brought the outside, the police brutality from which he, Hill, was protected, inside, an outside from which all the other players too were protected. He brought it right into the locker room, making police brutality immanent, intimate, and in so doing Hill compelled a geopolitical triangulation among Orlando, Milwaukee, and Kenosha. By making police brutality a bubble issue, Hill transformed the bubble into an instrument that could be mobilized against police brutality. (How effective an instrument was a matter of concern for the players, already in a moral quandary about their decision to play after George Floyd's murder.) If it is police brutality that was "breaking in," then it was black athletic resistance, metonymized as/in Hill, that was "breaking out." In "breaking out" black athletes were reaching out to black America, writ large, making manifest their support for the cause: ending police brutality and securing social justice for all marginalized and oppressed Americans.

George Hill turned the bubble inside out. He made the bubble face outward, he made the bubble stand before the world. Or, from a different vantage point, he inserted—with the force that is per-sonal conviction—the world into the bubble. Either way, what Hill succeeded in doing was to, if the pun might be permitted, burst the bubble. It does not take a reigning MVP (Giannis) or an NBA leg-end (LeBron) to burst the bubble. It only requires, it turns out, your average NBA guard to make (circumscribed) utopia of a piece with the dystopia raging at its doorstep; almost literally, in the case of Kenosha's proximity to Milwaukee, if not Orlando. To burst the bub-ble, a thirteen-year NBA veteran with a strong commitment to social justice will do as well as his Defensive Player of the Year teammate.

Cometh the hour, cometh the black athlete. Cometh the black ath-lete who is not a household name. "What's my name?" "George Hill."

No Surprise

In truth, Hill's teammates should not have been surprised that it was he who broke ranks, if only momentarily. While the injured Kyrie Irving (Brooklyn Nets) made clear his opinion that the NBA should not resume because of the racist conditions extant in American life,[8] the WNBA's Natasha Cloud (Washington Mystics) is the only player from either league who chose not to go into the (WNBA's) bubble at the IMG Academy in Brandenton, Florida, in order to concentrate on her social justice activism.[9] Hill, on the other hand, elected to go to Orlando.

It did not, however, take him long to voice his ambivalence. Responding to the Kenosha police shooting of Jacob Blake, Hill could barely contain his anger. Some of it, no doubt, can only be described as public self-recrimination:

> First of all, we shouldn't have come to this damn place to be honest.
>   Coming here just took all the focal points off what the issues are.
> But we're here. It is what it is. We can't do anything from right here.
> But definitely when it's all settled, some things need to be done.[10]

After the murder of George Floyd by Derek Chauvin of the Minneapolis Police Department, many NBA and WNBA players—Cloud and Beal among them—had marched against police brutality. What Hill's reflection suggest, more than anything, is a sense of location-imposed helplessness—"we're here," and from "right here" "We can't do anything." As NBA players, they have made themselves captive. More than that, they have made themselves helpless. From "right here" the NBA players understand them-

---

8. A number of NBA players, among them Bradley Beal, DeMarcus Cousins, Trevor Ariza, Kelly Oubre, Thabo Sefalosha, who chose not to enter the bubble because of health (fear of contracting Covid-19; injuries) or family concerns. Several of those who opted out cited the importance of being with their families. One of those players was Avery Bradley, a guard with the L.A. Lakers, thereby passing up his chance to win an NBA title.

9. Dorothy J. Gentry, "Two Athletes United as Partners for Justice," *New York Times*, September 3, 2020. Gentry offers an insight into the rare collaboration between the city of Washington's Wizards (NBA) and the WNBA franchise. Gentry focuses on the close relationship between Cloud and the Wizards' Bradley Beal.

10. https://basketball.realgm.com/wiretap/259324/George-Hill-We-Shouldnt-Have-Come-To-This-Damn-Place-To-Be-Honest.

selves to be of no use to their community. How could they stop police brutality from "right here?"

Hill's helplessness also echoes in a different register. It voices the unspeakable truth that the seven bullets that paralyzed Jacob Blake came too soon, much too soon, after George Floyd's death. As such, it might also simply be a sign of ontological exhaustion. As in: this has happened again. As in: this has happened again as it has before. It is out of this anger and helplessness, one suspects, that some NBA players in the bubble chose to have "Enough" inscribed on the back of their jerseys, where their names would ordinarily have appeared.

It is with this understanding, the regularity of black death by white police officers, that Hill's self-recrimination becomes audible. "Coming here just took all the focal points off what the issues are." By having decided to play basketball, the players may have rendered themselves politically helpless and ineffective. By playing in the bubble they allowed for the "focal point" to be lost in the routine, albeit a utopian one, of the NBA playoffs. That is, it is the game itself that came to take precedence. Once more, as it always is, the focus is on the game.

In truth, however, Hill was caught in an odd conundrum. And it is not an entirely self-negating conundrum. While he could not leave the bubble without absenting himself from his team (he would have to quarantine himself after he returned, by which time the Bucks might very well have lost; at the very least they would have had to make do without a player), it is precisely his ability to articulate the restrictions of his voluntary encampment that allows him the platform from which to vent his frustrations. It is also the threat of bursting the bubble that made his action so salient. That made of George Hill *George Hill*. The threat of bursting the bubble made the (outside) world look to the bubble for political direction. For guidance.

In his ambivalence, Hill gave life to political possibilities that would not, under normal circumstances, have had such resonance. The intensity of that resonance—everyone ventured an opinion on what the Hill-led Bucks did, from Trump to the opinion-makers on cable TV—is precisely how Hill and his colleagues were able to escape the captivity of the bubble. It was their very "captivity" that provided a platform and, as such, amplified the antiracist and anti-police brutality message. Critical to the resonance was the reality of shared encampment. All the players were gathered together in one place. Whether or not they understood it as such, theirs was heard as a single, unified voice. No matter, as we will see, the inaccuracy of that perception. Through encampment, the "focal point" was sharpened.

Nineteenth century American utopianists, one and all, subscribed to the logic of exemplarity. Fourierists, Owenites, and the Perfectionists believed—and believed deeply—that if they could model the ideal community, their neighbors, no matter how skeptical, disapproving, or antagonistic they might initially be, would see, through utopian example, what a desirable mode of being utopianism offered.

The as-yet unconverted would follow suit. It was a matter of time.

Life in the Shaker village, the Fourierist phalanx, Brook Farm, or New Harmony, would show itself to be a preferable mode of existence.

The Oneida Mansion House as but the first instantiation of Mansion Houses that spring up across the county, the state, the entirety of the United States. A new way to live.

In truth, only a few newcomers—or outsiders—swelled the utopian ranks, but not in any great number.

No matter. The belief persisted that the truth emanating from a New Harmony was an example to and for all of humanity. Owen, Noyes, and their like had simply gotten there earlier.

Out of their Disney-cum-utopian location, the NBA players fashioned, out of racial affinity, a profound sense of injustice and a deep sense of sociopolitical accountability, themselves as an exemplary community for a white majority country at war with its black and brown populations.

An echo of "Follow the Deer" reverberates.

The truth emanating from the bubble was that what-was would no longer be tolerated. The bubble, if only in reformist terms, agitated for what-should-be. Jayson Tatum's nostalgia as the utopian inscription of the bubble. The bubble, Tatum's short-lived experience showed him, was not only its own kind of possibility. It was, for him (and possibly not only as a professional athlete), a way to live.[11]

In the World Interior of Capital is Peter Sloterdijk's call for the revitalization of grand narratives, notwithstanding—as Sloterdijk recognizes—the failure of such narratives. However, read within our context, it is difficult not to ignore the undercurrents of a utopian inclination. Sloterdijk's argument is for a return to philosophy itself as the creation of a grand narrative. "Has thinking," Sloterdijk wonders, "not always meant taking on the challenge that the excessive would appear concretely before us?"[12] To "think" for what-must-be, no matter the enormity of the "challenge" that confronts. "Thinking" for what-must-be is for Sloterdijk necessarily a communal project, a "dwelling" (a concept he borrows from Heidegger) in which shared experience, shared protection, and shared responsibility for the maintenance of the dwelling is the order of the day. "Dwelling," Sloterdijk writes, "creates an immune system of repeatable gestures; through successful habituation, it combines being-relieved with being-burdened by clear tasks."[13] In the bubble NBA players were "relieved" of certain mundane "tasks": only, that is, to find themselves tasked—"being-burdened"—with a set of responsibilities that proved themselves to be far more onerous, many times more demanding. Such is the work of "successful habituation." To learn to live, differently. That is what Jayson Tatum learned. Learned, and, because he became habituated to it,

11. Here Tatum captures something of the spirit of Christopher Castiglia's argument, in his advocating for a critique of hope, that a "critique of the present" amounts to the envisioning of a "more desirable future." Castiglia, *The Practices of Hope: Literary Criticism in Disenchanted Times* (New York: New York University Press, 2017), 2.

12. Peter Sloterdijk, *In the World Interior of Capital: For a Philosophical Theory of Globalization*, trans. Wieland Hoban (Malden, Mass.: Polity, 2017), 5.

13. Sloterdijk, 256.

yearned-for on finding himself cast back into the world beyond the confines of the bubble.

What NBA players approached, in Silver's recollection, with uncertainty and no small amount of foreboding, revealed itself as preferable to what-was. After the bubble, would normal NBA life ever be enough? If the NBA players were exemplary in their truth, their critique of U.S. racism, were they not also the first practitioners of a utopian life for professional athletes? Professional athletes working—that is, going about their job, playing basketball—in conjunction with a socioeconomic structure, if not of their making, then certainly partly born out of their professional necessity?

Because of how publicly Hill chafed at the (social, political) isolation that the bubble imposed on the players, because he was so forthright about his ambivalence, because his self-recrimination (which was individual but contained a collective sting, have no doubt of that) was so palpable, his decision not to play should not have come as a surprise. And yet it did.

And because it surprised everybody, maybe even Budenholzer when Hill communicated his decision privately, Hill's decision had the effect of reverberating so that it discombobulated public discourse about police brutality entirely. Threw everything into question. In fact, by "unsettling" things, by making everything more turbulent rather than waiting until things "settled down," Hill had already begun to "get things done." Hill's inner—and visible, articulated—turmoil had the effect of shaking things up. Hill made, if only for a moment, the nation grapple with the ugly racism of police brutality. He gave the brutal fact of white police violence against black bodies a new discursive intensity. He maybe even gave it an ethical life. This is what happens when a black athlete speaks up, as it were, by sitting out.

Because of what followed in the wake of his decision, the force of Hill's determined withdrawal may have surprised everyone. George Hill not least of all.

Strange things happen in the bubble.

In the bubble, because of the bubble, the NBA—in concert with the

WNBA—shows itself to be the most progressive force in American political life.

The bubble, an artificial space, a space for artifice. Without artifice there can be no utopia.

Once more, a black athlete takes up the work of making America account for itself, even when powerful constituencies refuse to confront the truth of American racism.

3. Out of One, Many

WHEN HILL TOLD HIS TEAMMATES that he would not play on August 26, they all decided to support his decision. Sterling Brown was the first to voice his assent.

For Hill and his Bucks teammates, however, an individual refusal that became, as we shall see, a potential forfeit that morphed into a league-wide boycott, was not enough:

> Following their walkout, Bucks players, led by Hill and his teammate Sterling Brown, called elected officials in Wisconsin to take concrete steps to hold the police officers accountable for how they treated Mr. Blake.
> "For this to occur, it's imperative for the Wisconsin State Legislature to reconvene after months of inaction and take up meaningful measures to address issues of police brutality and criminal justice reform," Mr. Hill said.[1]

Following what happened to Jacob Blake, Hill, Brown, and the Bucks had had enough. "Enough." A statement of political will. A Nietzschean-inflected decision: "Willing emancipateth: that is the true doctrine of will and emancipation."[2] A declaration intended to end things as they were. During the playoffs, Danny Green, then of the L.A. Lakers (before being traded to the Philadelphia 76ers)

1. Marc Stein, Sopan Deb, and Alan Blinder, "With Walkouts, N.B.A. Players Jolt Pro Sports," *New York Times,* August 28, 2020.
2. Nietzsche, *Beyond Good and Evil,* 92.

and Amir Coffey of the Houston Rockets, had "How Many More" inscribed on the back of their jerseys. A question that defies the rules of grammar by refusing to append a question mark, thus converting the question that is not a question into a declarative that demands address.

But "Enough" also as a critique framed by erasure; that is, for everything we say, we leave several things unsaid. That is, when will "Enough" pose itself as a term of exclusion—which athletes from historically disenfranchised constituencies are not participating in or excluded from this struggle? If so, why? Can this question, which should include but not be limited to issues such as gender inequality and homophobia in sport, be taken up even as the protest against racism and police brutality continues? These are, after all, questions that bear on a different mode of exclusion. Is the issue not now both "Enough" and "More"? Can this moment, this movement against police brutality, afford to satisfy itself that, as it is now constituted, it is indeed "Enough"?

What is more, is it not also high time that we recognize the limitations of this call for justice with its focus on, in the main, democracy as defined by electoral politics and its determination to remake policing? These are undoubtedly necessary and important goals. Indeed, especially as it pertains to the latter, more often than not a matter of life or death. As such it must be supported. This is one rail of dual power.

However, if the political—that is, the state and representation as the only horizon of possibility—remains the dominant mode of thinking within the ranks of those resisting racism, police brutality, gender discrimination (in its several articulations), then this circumscription of what it means to be in the world democratically is a priori curtailed. Equality of/in representation is no guarantee of equal access to resources and certainly does not safeguard labor against the predations of capital.

The other rail of dual power is the one which calls for the radical reorganization of society.

Life in the bubble—be that Hill's or Osaka's—as the paradigmatic starting point of thinking for a new society. New modes of human re-

lationships, one in which mutual dependency and intense competition coexist, while everyone shares in the risks and everyone is guaranteed housing, healthcare, food and, yes, recreation. Fun. Downtime. But also, and here the NBA's "campus" model in Orlando is instructive, a time to learn and a time to teach.

Inside the bubble John Lucas, an assistant coach for the Houston Rockets and a longtime advocate against substance abuse, took a moment to remind the players of the dangers of excessive alcohol consumption. CJ McCollum, the Portland Trail Blazers guard, remembers this moment: "When his speech concluded, the players all erupted and gave Lucas a standing ovation."[3] Lucas, a recovering substance abuser, spoke from experience. A time to play, a time to relax, a time to be instructed.

Reformism and the inclining toward utopianism in a necessarily tense coexistence.

A critical part of which will be that black professional athletes will have to directly confront their class privilege, as distinct from their racial vulnerability.

Carmelo Anthony, McCollum's Blazers' teammate, taken aback during the players' meeting to discuss the effects of Hill and the Bucks' decision where, for some of his colleagues, financial considerations trumped political ones, remarked, biblically, "Money is the root of all evil."[4] An evil from which no one is exempt.

Who among Anthony's colleagues will commit to the redistribution of resources?

In fact, the answer might be already to hand: on the jersey, of an opponent, who declares, unwittingly, in response to, we are in agreement, Green and Coffey's declarative: "Enough." The number of black victims of police brutality has long since reached its limit. Enough. No More.

However, No More is a priori overwritten with a certain black futility and hopelessness. The intention to terminate police brutality

3. Rooks, "Most Magical Place on Earth," 119.
4. Rooks, 119.

is already inscribed with the expectation of further acts of police violence against black bodies. "Enough," which adorned (during the playoffs) the jerseys of, among others, Ivica Zubac (Clippers), Frank Mason (Bucks) and Brad Wannamaker (Boston Celtics), is the declaration: Who is next? That is the presumption. An inevitable presumption. Trayvon Martin was not enough. Sandra Bland was not enough. Michael Brown . . . Freddie Gray . . . Breonna Taylor . . . Enough is the ever-receding sightline where black hope dies, only to be rekindled by and because of the memory. After Breonna Taylor comes Ahmaud Arbery, after George Floyd comes Daunte Wright, so that once more, as if for the first time, "Enough" regains its vigor, inscribed with a fresh (but not unfamiliar) intensity and a reanimated political will as an antipolice brutality rallying cry. It is always only a matter of "When?" the next black body is victimized.

A part of me is uncertain, Nip, when the critique "systemic racism" is invoked. Not because I disagree with the analysis, because the "culture" of policing in the United States bears out the truth of the critique. It is, rather, because a part of me, when we see repeated acts of police brutality against black bodies, is pushed to the outer limits of reasoning to produce an answer. At my nadir, the best—or, worst, as the case might be—I can do is offer pure sadism as an explanation, in no small measure because of policemen such as Officer Weber of the Minneapolis Police Department:

> *The cell phone recording went viral around the world: a twenty-four-year veteran of the Minneapolis Police Department threatening to break the leg of a teenager if he didn't cooperate when stopped by police in March 2015.*
>
> *"If you fuck with me, I'm gonna break your leg before you even get a chance to run," Officer Roderic Weber told one of the four Somali American teens in the car.*
>
> *"I don't screw around."*
>
> *"Can you tell me why I'm being arrested?" one of the teens asked.*
>
> *"Because I feel like arresting you," Weber replied.*[5]

5. https://sahanjournal.com/police/minneapolis-police-depart-ment-black-hawk-down-somali-teens/.

Sadism of the, in its etymological sense, masochistic variety, inflected with the mindset of the white American police officer: the sadist is that person who has the power to inflect, for no reason, none whatsoever, cruelty, and even extreme cruelty, upon those over whom it exercises power. The logic is uncomplicated. The sadistic masochist requires no rationale: "Because I feel like arresting you."[6] To cause pain or degradation on the other in order, we can safely assume, to provide the police officer with the gratification that only the random, unchecked exercise of power can provide. A perverse mode of being in the world, no doubt limned by a psychosexual element. By no means, however, an unusual motivation for Officer Weber and his ilk.

To behave sadistically whether or not there are black kids in the car, kids about to be traumatized by police brutality. Jacob Blake's kids were in the car with him.

In case you think me excessive, son, I watched a YouTube video in which a white Uber driver refuses to stop recording an aggressive, belligerent police officer who is arresting his passenger. It turns out that the Uber driver is also an attorney, and, as such, pronounces himself familiar with his right to keep recording.[7]

I know, you and I know, that had the Uber driver been black, his fate would have been different. Chances are he would not have lived to tell the tale. Instead, he might have simply been recording his own death.

America's two justice systems at work.

Racism? Sadism? A deep, historic hatred for black life? I am reluctant to settle on a single rationale but I doubt I can get much beyond sadism. After that, well, now there's a rabbit hole I'd rather not go down.

So you will have to accept sadism as the sign of my hopelessness. The brutal limits of my reason.

6. See also https://minnesotareformer.com/2020/12/15/the-bad-cops-how-minneapolis-protects-its-worst-police-officers-until-its-too-late/.

7. https://www.bing.com/videos/search?q=you-tube+video+of+the+white+attorney+who+kept+filming+his+stop+by+the+police&docid=608045314865369022&mid=35461F2E-A7167E2F75CA35461F2EA7167E2F75CA&view=detail&FORM=VIRE.

4. Reforming the Unreformable

GEORGE HILL still believes in structural accountability. For that I am grateful. He is giving you something to hold onto, Ezra. He believes that reform must be a priority. Beginning with Rusten Sheskey—a forlorn hope, it turns out. George Hill's jersey read, presciently (to use the term loosely; there is nothing prescient about anticipating the next black death by police brutality), "Justice now."

There is a moment in Fredric Jameson's essay on utopia when he focuses on "omnipresent corruption."[1] In the process, Jameson argues that "omnipresent corruption" is at work in the "system at large, which is, in any case, too enormous and too complex to be susceptible to any decisive tinkerings which might improve it, let alone lead to something you could truly call systemic change."[2]

As a slogan, "Enough," as much as "Education reform" (and, in all probability, every one of the other inscriptions that adorned the players' jerseys), is a reformist inadequacy designed to meet only the most pressing demands of our moment.

All the while the Leninist injunction obtains so "Enough" is decidedly not enough.

As Alex S. Vitale argues in The End of Policing, *all talk about the reform of policing must be abandoned, for no reason other than it is*

1. Fredric Jameson, "An American Utopia," in *An American Utopia: Dual Power and the Universal Army*, ed. Slavoj Žižek (New York: Verso, 2015), 3.
2. Jameson, 3.

an impossibility. And even if it were possible, there is no political will for it. And even if it were possible, the powerful police unions would do everything possible to oppose such policies. They would surely work to obstruct "meaningful" reforms and/or to delay its implementation.

After all, the Minneapolis Police union, as reactionary as they come, fought tenaciously to keep Officer Weber in its ranks.

This is the truth upon which the "Defund the Police" movement is founded, a truth as controversial in some liberal circles as it used as a blunt instrument in reactionary ones. Historically grounded, it is not surprising that Vitale's work anticipated, symptomatically rendered, Ahmaud Arbery, Breonna Taylor . . . Daunte Wright. Published in 2017, three years before George Floyd's murder, Vitale is trenchantly clear: "We don't need empty police reforms; we need a robust democracy that gives people the capacity to demand of their government and themselves real, nonpunitive solutions to their problems."[3]

These "problems" include, as we well know, inequality in education as well as an economic system intent on either extracting maximum value from labor or, worse(?), condemning those superfluous to capitalism's needs to a Hobbesian fate. An unsightly fate, best kept out of sight. (A recent study determines the United States as the most unequal of Western democracies.)[4] Poorly educated minorities, homelessness, mental illness, the working poor and their lumpen cousins are not "problems" policing is either designed or committed to solving. Working to end white police brutality is what today demands. Such a goal requires opening up to the possibility of society free from policing entirely. What is necessary, then, is the imagining of a tomorrow that breaks entirely with the political logic—that is, with the reformist premises and constraints—that obtain today.

Our thinking of how to reorder the world must begin with the likes of Vitale and other critics of policing (Radley Balko, Joseph J. Ested, Jennifer E. Cobbina, Angela J. Hattery, and Earl Smith) who

3. Alex S. Vitale, *The End of Policing* (New York: Verso, 2017), 30.
4. See https://www.npr.org/2021/01/04/953146884/eurasia-group-the-biggest-global-risks-for-2021.

demonstrate, each in their own register, the futility of the reformist argument. A crucial component of the utopian project for Jameson is its capacity for self-reflexivity. Utopia as an unfinished or incompletable undertaking, a project in need of constant renovation and rethinking.[5] *In the terms offered by William Godwin* (An Enquiry Concerning Political Justice) *and Rousseau* (Discourse on the Origin of Inequality), *utopia as the project of "perfectibility." To this end, let us aphorize Godwin's position: in order to secure the "general good of the species" we must "reconcile" ourselves to the "desirableness of a government of the simplest construction."*[6] *Something on the order of More's Utopia: a democratically organized society with few rules.*

An odd place too, one where gold has no value. Gold is the stuff that kids play with in Utopia. One wonders what gold-ringed and necklaced professional athletes might make of such a prospect, such an inversion of values.

So rather than take the court for their playoff game, the Bucks players were talking with the Wisconsin attorney-general about how to ensure that Sheskey would be charged and brought to justice. It did not happen. (All the more reason to abandon reformism.) To ensure that the judicial process would be expeditious as well as just,

---

5. It is telling that Rosa Luxemburg, for all her opposition to utopianism, maintains a flexibility to context—"There is no key in any socialist party program or textbook." Luxemburg, "The Russian Revolution," in *The Rosa Luxemburg Reader,* ed. Peter Hudis and Kevin B. Anderson (New York: Monthly Review Press, 2004), 306. Declaring an openness to experimentation, spontaneous and creative responses to on-the-ground conditions critical to the socialist project, Luxemburg maintains that such an approach is "not a shortcoming but rather the very thing that makes scientific socialism superior to the utopian varieties" (306). Where Luxemburg discerns the need for clear distinctions between "scientific socialism" and utopianism, Jameson eschews revolutionary dogmatism in favor of releasing utopianism into a flurry of possibility, no matter the difficulties that may be encountered, regardless of the programmatic purity that is either present or absent. Critical to Jameson is the response that the conjuncture demands.

6. William Godwin, *An Enquiry concerning Political Justice* (Oxford: Oxford University Press, 2013), 4, 5.

the "Deer" were not asking the Magic players to join them in boycotting the game. Neither were the Bucks players asking for a postponement, which would allow for the game, in a series the Bucks were
leading three games to one, to be played at a later date, although this
is how things would eventually turn out. No. The Milwaukee Bucks
players, in taking their stand, were making a clear statement: they
were willing to forfeit their game. That is, in not taking the court,
they were announcing their willingness to concede the game to the
Magic. In doing so, the Bucks players were contravening the terms
of their own union—the National Basketball Players Association
(NBPA), which has an agreement with the league owners that pro-
hibits striking. And, striking is what the Bucks were doing, although
the preferred nomenclature was "boycott."

The Bucks were striking, in the strict labor sense, by withholding their labor, but also striking insofar as they sought to strike a
blow against police brutality by absenting their bodies from public
view. The Bucks were bringing attention to systemic American racism by, to mix sports metaphors, giving their particular inflection
to the baseball phrase "striking out," a term that itself is redolent
with both "failure"—the inability to make contact, as in a baseball player missing a pitch, strike three, and is called "out"—and
violence—to act physically, with malicious intent, against another.
That, however, would be misleading, because what the Bucks were
doing was striking out (speaking determinedly, and angrily too,
one imagines, against racial injustice)—by not playing—against
the horrific police violence meted out, in this specific instance, to
Jacob Blake.

*If any among us had doubts about the depth of white racist sen-
timent among police officers, then such hesitation or ambivalence
was done away with, rudely, by the Trump-inspired insurrection of
January 6, 2021. The significant number of law enforcement officials
involved in storming of the capital laid bare the extent of white supremacist thinking in the ranks of the police. It should have surprised
no one. Instead, it should have told us what we should already know:
there can be no reforming the police.*

If any of us had any doubts, the shooting of Adam Toledo, a thirteen-year-old Latino boy by a Chicago police officer, should have put paid to that. A thirteen-year-old boy, in a dark alley, holding up his hands, surrendering. Shot, once, fatally, by officer Eric Stillman. The Chicago police union chief defended the officer.[7]

Here too, however, the strategy that is dual power has a role to play. In April 2021, the Maryland legislature voted to repeal its police Bill of Rights,[8] *overturning a veto by Governor Larry Hogan. The Bill of Rights was one of three pieces of legislation repealed, of which the police Bill of Rights is salient because it provides police officers with immunity from investigation and prosecution for actions committed during the course of duty. The Bill extends to police officers due process privileges not extended to ordinary civilians.*

The repeal by the Maryland legislature should not, however, be understood as standing in opposition to the defund the police movement, but as its corollary. Undoing undue police privilege and protection before the law is what representative politics can do. It is appropriate that Maryland should be the first state to repeal a police Bill of Rights because it was the first state to enact such a bill, in 1974.

The Maryland repeal might, or might not, mark the limit of representative politics' ability to reign in police brutality and make it accountable to the citizenry. What it cannot do, however, is solve the problem.

(In fairness, however, let us score this as a win for reformism. With the precondition, of course, that such a reformist victory recognizes itself as temporary and as furthering the cause of its ultimate negation.)

What the imposition of restraint on police violence can do, however, is open up a pathway to thinking how a society can organize itself in such a way that obviates the need for policing. And it raises the difficult

7. https://www.msn.com/en-us/news/us/sean-hannity-slammed-for-calling-adam-toledo-a-13-year-old-man/ar-BB1fIAwp?ocid=spartan-dhp-feeds.

8. https://wtop.com/maryland/2021/04/maryland-general-assembly-overturns-governors-vetoes-of-police-reform-bills/.

question of how to ensure nonviolent, harmonious, and conflictual living (utopia does not seek to do away with conflict; instead, it works to organize those propensities) without the threat of repressive force. How can everyone live safely without a repressive apparatus?

An onerous undertaking, to be sure, but a necessary one.

Especially necessary in light of the history of policing, a history of violence against vulnerable constituencies that obtains with a virulence in our moment.

Repealing the police Bill of Rights as the first step toward living in a safe, police-free utopia. Appropriating the progressive tendencies in representative politics in order to undo it completely.

Consolidating dual power into a singularly utopian project.

In acting unilaterally, the Bucks players were going against their own union and against their own league. The NBA is a black majority league, in terms of the players if not majority ownership, which, it must be said (especially under the leadership of Adam Silver,[9] the NBA commissioner), has historically been the league most sympathetic to and attuned to the struggles of their players—and, by extension, their communities. (The NBA and the WNBA are by far the most progressive of the four major sports leagues—baseball, basketball, football and ice hockey.) That the Bucks, moved to inaction by Hill, were acting as a sovereign political entity was obvious—perhaps more obvious in retrospect than in the moment itself; still, no matter—because their opponents were not alerted to their decision. The vanguardist Bucks led from the front. And they did so out of a geopolitical and, if you insist, personal, imperative. Jacob Blake lived within the larger environs of Milwaukee, their city. It was, as they correctly understood it, a responsibility that geography had determined fell to them. They, the Milwaukee Bucks, before anyone else, had to act. Not only them, in the end, but

9. https://www.msn.com/en-us/sports/nba/adam-silver-final-ly-discusses-nba-boycotts-i-understand-the-pain-anger-and-frustration/ar-BB18tcyh?ocid=spartan-dhp-feeds.

they had to lead. It was up to the Deer to lead their community in a moment of racist Fear.

"Systemic change" cannot be achieved in the current conditions because, as Jameson puts it, staying with his theme of political corruption, "representative democracy is irreparably corrupt and incapable of fulfilling its promises."[10]

At the very least, then, what Jameson offers is the need to reflect upon the insufficiency of "Enough" and how such a constitutive insufficiency demands a confrontation with the failures of previously "unfulfilled promise(s)."

However, it is also important to acknowledge the role that the Leninist concept of "dual power" plays in Jameson's diagnosis. That is, as much as the historic limitations of representative democracy must be kept in the forefront of our thinking, this does not mean that George Hill and the Bucks should not have made, in that moment, and in its aftermath, should not continue to make, demands upon the powers that be in Wisconsin. (And they did, as shown below.) It simply means that such a "representation" to power is but one of the two axes along which the "politics of the instant" run.[11] *Dual power demands that two struggles be conducted simultaneously.*

That is, it is necessary to make demands on the apparatus of power in Wisconsin while also asking seriously, and without preconception, What might be enough? How do movements that engage in "politics of the instant" want to organize—rather than only reorganize—society? How can a "politics of the instant," what Michael Hardt and Antonio Negri have named the "multitude" (as Jameson reminds us), organize itself so that it can "tinker" with institutions as they are, but only with the intention of doing away with the society as we know it entirely? "Enough," then, as the place where a utopian imagining—or any other imagining—has its genesis rather than marking a terminal (political) ambition.

10. Jameson, "An American Utopia," 5.
11. Jameson, 13.

From the vantage point of the still unaware Orlando Magic, just going about their usual shoot-about routine, the terms of the "contest," to misrepresent the matter, went from the sloganistic, NBA-appropriate, "Fear the Deer" to the politically charged "Follow the Deer." That way, as indicated by the "Deer," lies the path to justice, beginning with ensuring that the appropriate punishment is meted out to Rusten Sheskey. Alas. In vain. It turns out.

Soon enough, the Magic players were informed of their opponents' decision, to which they assented. Consequently, all of the NBA games for August 26 were postponed. Following that, after a players meeting (and in consultation with the NBA), all of the games for the 27th were similarly put on hold. (Play resumed on Saturday, August 29, with the Bucks sweeping aside the Magic.) Player-coaching staff-commissioner solidarity prevailed, if only after several hours of tumultuous discussion among the players. NBPA solidarity, under the leadership of Chris Paul (then of the Houston Rockets, now of the Phoenix Suns), forged out of a series of difficult conversations amongst the players in the NBA's Covid-19-imposed "bubble," dictated that no forfeiture was necessary. (Conversations that were mediated, in their most fractious moments, by Michael Jordan, the Chicago Bulls legend who is now the majority owner of the Charlotte Hornets.) However, before the agreement was reached to continue playing, the Lakers (led by LeBron James) and the Clippers were in fact willing to go further. (This after voicing their displeasure at the Bucks' unilateral action.) The Lakers and the Clippers, two of the teams fancied to win the 2020 NBA championship, wanted to end the NBA season entirely. The two-day postponement represented a compromise, part of which was a commitment to keep social justice in the forefront of the remainder of the NBA postseason.

Out of the specter of forfeiture, which itself marks a willingness on the part of the Bucks players to sacrifice professionally (protesting police brutality is more important than playing the game of basketball), emerged the athletes' movement against racism and injustice.

Let us propose "Enough" as the first articulation of dual power. Black athletes, led by the Bucks and supported by a host of NBA teams such as the L.A. Lakers (under the impetus provided by LeBron James), the Charlotte Hornets, the Houston Rockets, and the Miami Heat, made their organizational facilities available as polling places.[12] By actively encouraging their fan base to vote, the NBA, the WBNA, and the National Football League (NFL), inter alia, and the players union operated within the structures of power. They worked at the level of representative democracy, registering their opposition to Trump and his policies. In pursuing this mode of political intervention, the NBA and its players worked actively to offset the Trump regime's constant efforts to suppress minority voter turnout. It worked. Trump was defeated in the 2020 presidential election. This campaign by the NBA, WBNA, the NFL, and so on showed itself important within the context of U.S. electoral politics. Reformism as necessary both in the moment of the now and, in all probability, for the foreseeable future.

Outside their NBA bubble, the world around them seemed to be everywhere aflame. Literally aflame in Kenosha, where buildings were set alight, where police clashed with protesters as soon as darkness set in and the state-imposed curfew was ignored, and while the Kenosha police stood idly by while a gun-wielding teenager, Kyle Rittenhouse of Antioch, Illinois, strutted through Kenosha's streets shooting and killing two people and badly wounding a third. Rittenhouse found himself hailed appreciatively by passing cops and thrown a bottle of water for refreshment, by the cops, into the bargain.[13] Literally aflame in already-much traumatized Minneapolis,

---

12. See the following for a complete list of NBA venues to be used as polling places: https://www.cbssports.com/nba/news/nba-polling-places-which-arenas-will-serve-as-voting-sites-for-november-election-after-player-protests/.

13. Continuing in this trend, police officers have been among the key contributors to Rittenhouse's defense funds. https://www.msn.com/en-us/news/us/opinion-surprising-to-nobody-black-kyle-rittenhouse-receives-donations-from-cops-and-public-officials-according-to-data-breach/ar-BB-1fLc87?ocid=spartan-dhp-feeds.

still trying to emerge into some form of public life after the May 2020 murder of George Floyd, where the death of a man on August 26, 2020, sparked conflicting rumors—suicide, homicide, police brutality. In a country on the edge, Minneapolis was perhaps the most finely balanced, ready to tip over, once more, into civil unrest, understandable, given how high tensions were running. The flames of racial animus were further fanned, once again, as they had been ever since Donald Trump took office, from the White House, playing host to the Republican national convention, from whence nary a word emerged on the shooting of Jacob Blake and the vigilante justice of Kyle Rittenhouse.

5. *Nur ein Gott kann uns jetzt Retten*

IN HIS FAMOUS 1966 *Der Spiegel* interview, published (per his wishes) only after his death (1976), Martin Heidegger, with the memory (Hiroshima, Nagasaki) and prospect (mutually assured destruction) of nuclear disaster very much on his mind, declared: *Nur ein Gott kann uns jetzt retten* (Only a god can save us now). This phrase summarizes, succinctly, provocatively and resonantly, Heidegger's longstanding fear of and overall dislike for technology. Technology could destroy like no other force in history, leaving human *Sein* (Being and being) nothing but a toxic dump. Into the hands of "*a* god"—*ein Gott*—Heidegger, a Catholic until his dying day (his long struggle with the church notwithstanding), commended the human race.

Out of the Milwaukee Bucks' locker room, closed to the world, shut off from the media and other prying eyes and pricked ears, emerged a rather more hopeful iteration of Heidegger's injunction. Heidegger's was, with global destruction a real possibility, a desperate plea for some form of human intervention (against technology). Heidegger's was a call for help in the project to stay technology and, for him, its deleterious effect. It was also, given Heidegger's role in providing some philosophical ballast and solace for 1930s National Socialism, a barely disguised cry—but muted by his philosophical acuity—for some form of (individual, personal) absolution from history.

The bubble is no insulation against police brutality.

In the bubble things might even become more intense.

Life, as players such as Paul George (L.A. Clippers) attest (as he grappled with psychological issues), can prove debilitating in the bubble.

The bubble is no match for black athletic anger.

"Something is breaking in and something is breaking out."

From out of the bubble in Orlando, Heidegger's phrase was assumed a distinctly more responsible—so I like to insist—iteration. This variation, the product of George Hill's formidable will (which Nietzsche might have admired), marked that moment when a new and determined incarnation of black athletic intellectuality came into being. A black conscience, a deep-thinking consciousness of what it means to be black in America. An attempt to forge a conscientious and felicitous relationship to the moment at hand, to the demands of a historic conjuncture. In pivotal historical moments, these have all been key attributes displayed by radicalized and radicalizing black athletes. This is a feature that marks black American athletes from Jack Johnson to John Carlos, from Jim Brown to Serena Williams.

In this regard, the work of constructing the second axis of dual power—how to organize society differently, how to construct an entirely new future, how to achieve greater perfectibility, in short—should be taken up by all for whom a radical imagining has long been the stuff of their, shall we say, dreams?

This second axis, Lenin's revolution—the soviets, revolutionary councils, collective labor, redistribution of wealth, guaranteed minimum annual wage, universal health care, equal education for all, and so on—should fall to those for who, while engaged in determinedly pursuing the "politics of the instant," recognize, either intellectually or intuitively (it matters not how this insight is achieved), the limits of representation (because it will reach that terminus we know as electoral politics) and, in so doing, reach for what is not-yet but what can, through a racial imagining, come-to-be.

6. Strange Things Happen in the Bubble

HILL AND THE BUCKS, through their silent withdrawing, made evident, once more, that only a black athlete can save us now.

Heidegger's injunction, famous as it may be, *Nur ein Gott kann uns jetzt retten* is, of historical and philosophical necessity, vague, and, in truth, rather hopeless.

Nevertheless, like Heidegger, I cannot, as I have already said, pretend myself to be optimistic.

But in this moment, out of an admixture of desperation and with a profound regard for the tradition of transformative black athletes, all the while hedging my bets, it is patently obvious to me that only a black athlete can save us now. Heideggerian poetics in the service of the radical tradition that is black athletic activism. Muhammad Ali. Naomi Osaka. Lewis Hamilton.

Martin Heidegger was a keen football fan. In fact, it is said that he had a TV hidden in his office so that, in private, he could watch games. I am presuming, then, that Heidegger would join me in concluding that *nur ein schwarzer Sportler kann uns jetzt retten*.

In silence. Through resolute, unimpugnable, silence.

In the midst of all Trump's Sturm und Drang, his racist tweets, above the clamor and the endless analyses conducted across print, television and social media, it was the Bucks' absence and their silence that reverberated. That achieved resonance far beyond the confines of the bubble.

"Follow the Deer." Listen, if you can make yourself, attend to the incisiveness of the silence. Work your way past the cacophony. Try to hear the pain, injustice, anger, hopelessness, loss, and the crushing sense of precarity that is black life in America. Listen to how it is speaking. Silently. As a powerful silence. Hear what it is struggling to say.

Understand silence as a last resort.

Understand silence as a powerful point of political departure.

Silence is portentous, portentously loud, or so it has proved.

Strange things happen in the bubble. The strangest of which is not, but I would like to pretend that it is, anyway, that James Harden (then of the Houston Rockets, now of the Brooklyn Nets) does the unthinkable.

He plays defense.

No, James Harden plays effective, game-winning defense in Game 7 of a playoff series.

In the bubble (only in the bubble?), James Harden blocks a shot.

So strange it shocks the average NBA fan and it leaves Harden's opponent Chris Paul (Oklahoma Thunder) at a loss for words.

"James Harden? Defense?"

Only in the "bubble."

Just Grew

Within hours, the athletes' protest movement expanded. Rapidly. Across the United States. Within days, it found a receptive audience in Europe, particularly in England's Premier League where, one hopes, it will provoke a series of questions about the relationship between English-based players and those clubs that have American-based owners. (Arsenal, Aston Villa, Fulham, Liverpool, Manchester United, among others.)[1]

---

1. Fulham FC were relegated from the Premier League at the end of the 2020–21 season. They will now compete in the second tier of English

First things first, however. On August, 26, Milwaukee's Major League Baseball's (MLB) team the Brewers decided not to play their game against the Cincinnati Reds. The Seattle Mariners, in solidarity, decided that they would boycott their game against the Los Angeles Angels. The L.A. Dodgers, scheduled to play the San Francisco Giants, found their own George Hill in the person of Mookie Betts, their African American outfielder. Like Hill, Betts announced to his teammates that he would not play that night. Betts was publicly supported in his decision by the Dodgers' Curaçaoan closer, Kenley Jansen, L.A.'s ace starting pitcher Clayton Kershaw, who is white, and the team's African American manager, Dave Roberts. Kershaw is a pitcher notoriously wedded to routine. Kershaw is a player who prepares meticulously for each start and, as a consequence, does not like to have his routine disturbed. Nevertheless, scheduled to pitch against the Giants on the night of August 26th, Kershaw made it clear that his attachment to routine in no way compared to the conditions that Betts—and black people in America—confronted as their lived reality. Before the cameras, Kershaw thus took his place in support of Betts, Jansen, Roberts and the broader cause for racial justice.

Even my preternaturally hapless New York Metropolitans (Mets) showed themselves to be, for a moment, redeemable. When history demanded it, up stepped the Met's first baseman/outfielder, the African American Dominic Smith, as a spokesperson for the cause. At the postgame press conference on that August 26 evening, Smith, visibly moved, fighting back tears (not always successfully), lamented the condition of being black in America, unable to describe the pain that black people endure on a daily basis. The next day, the Mets and their opponents, the Florida Marlins, paused on their respective baselines for 42 seconds (in honor of Jackie Robinson, who wore number 42), took the field, then doffed their

---

football, a division known as the Championship. Some of these clubs are wholly owned by Americans, in others (Crystal Palace, West Ham, for example), Americans are minority owners.

caps to each other. There would be no play at Citi Field, the Mets' home ground, that day. A teary Smith was escorted off the field by his white team-mate, Pete Alonso, the first baseman—in fact, Alonso is the Mets' first-base prodigy who had displaced Smith from his position. Around MLB, that Thursday, August 27, several more teams refused to play their games—Philadelphia at Washington, Boston at Toronto, Minnesota at Detroit, Baltimore at Tampa Bay, and Oakland at the Texas Rangers. In so doing, they gave voice to their opposition to racism in America. Among the teams taking a principled position, it may be the Oakland A's who offered arguably the clearest denunciation of the status quo: "Social injustice and systemic racism have been part of the fabric of our lives for too long."[2]

2. Marc Stein, Sopan Deb, and Alan Blinder, "With Walkouts, N.B.A. Players Jolt Pro Sports," *New York Times,* August 28, 2020.

7. "Hey, Chicago, What Do You Say?"

NOT ALL MLB THE TEAMS, however, showed themselves possessed of a political consciousness. The New York Yankees (an establishment franchise, if there ever was one, from whom, quite frankly, I expect nothing, given their historic opposition to baseball integration in the pre-Jackie Robinson era and for years after), the Atlanta Braves (whose very name rankles; a team whose fans until recently still practiced the "tomahawk chop"), the St. Louis Cardinals (the franchise who exhibited the worst kind of racism to Jackie Robinson in the 1940s and '50s) just kept going, business as usual.

The Chicago Cubs, however, were especially disappointing.

One of their leaders, the African American outfielder, Jason Heyward, was left isolated by his teammates. When the Cubs so memorably won the World Series in 2016, it was Heyward who, during a rain delay in Game 7, the deciding game, gathered his teammates around him under the stands and rallied them to victory. On Valentine's Day 2018, when a gunman opened fire at Stoneman Douglas High School in Parkland, Florida, the Cubs first baseman, Anthony Rizzo, a Stoneman Douglas graduate, commendably, spoke in support of ending gun violence.[1] Not so here. Heyward was left to his own resources. Loyalty to clubhouse leaders has its limits. And

1. In July 2021 Rizzo was traded to the New York Yankees.

that limit is clearly marked: race. That is where solidarity ends for the Cubs in relation to Heyward. In this moment that old truism about Chicago's baseball divide rang true. The Sox, from the South Side, second stringers in their own city, feisty and combative, are the team that represents the city's racial minorities and white ethnics; the North Side's Cubbies, on the other hand, showed themselves to be the team of white suburbia.

A bitter pill for you to swallow, my son. Your maternal grandparents, mother, and brother are all lifelong Cubbie fans, and I know how difficult this is for them. "Hey Chicago, what do you say?"

Under these circumstances it is best to negate what the Cubbies faithful sing after a victory in Wrigleyville: Happy, jaunty renditions of "Go Cubs, Go Cubs, Go," can be heard along Waveland Avenue after a Cubs win. However much I try, "Don't Go Cubs, Don't Go," just doesn't have the same ring to it. In fact, rendered this way, it sounds silly, doesn't it? But maybe we can ask, "Hey, Chicago, what do you say?"

Still and all, I won't impose the Mets on you, son.

8. The WNBA Takes Its Stance

SHORTLY AFTER the Bucks made their announcement, the WNBA followed suit. The Washington Mystics, the L.A. Sparks, Atlanta Dream, and the Minnesota Lynx all took the court. However, instead of a basketball game, all the players took a knee. Then all four teams left the court. In the words of the Dream's Elizabeth Williams, "We stand in solidarity with our brothers in the NBA."[1] In many ways, the WNBA has not only "stood in solidarity," they have been a driving force for social justice. Twelve-year WNBA player Renee Montgomery of the Atlanta Dream opted out of the 2020 season in order to focus on political activism, following in the footsteps of the Maya Moore of the Minnesota Lynx, who chose the same path in 2019. A devout Christian, Moore saw it as her mission to pause her WNBA career in order to free Jonathan Irons, a black man who had been wrongfully imprisoned for more than twenty years. Only sixteen years old when he was arrested on burglary charges (home invasion) for a crime he did not commit, Irons was tried as an adult in 1998 in Missouri and sentenced to sixty-five years in prison. By an all-white jury, no less. In March 2020, thanks in no small measure to Moore's efforts, Irons was released.[2] (Moore and

1. https://www.chicagotribune.com/sports/breaking/ct-milwau-kee-bucks-protest-jacob-blake-20200826-gsgim3ogujcapnttgmyztkn-pny-story.html.
2. https://www.bbc.com/sport/basketball/53677658?ocid=uxbndl-bing.

Irons have subsequently gotten married and for her efforts Moore was announced as *Sports Illustrated*'s "Inspiration of the Year.") Moore's determination to secure justice for Irons demands that we, as Dave Zirin phrases it, "redouble our efforts to fight for the wrongly convicted, fight for alternatives to prison, and fight for a country that doesn't warehouse people who can't afford justice."[3] What Zirin's critique reminds is, rather chillingly, that Irons is the fortunate exception. He is the "lucky" one, those lost years of his life notwithstanding. Irons owes his release, in signal ways, to Christian fortuitousness. Before he was incarcerated, Irons had been a member of the church choir which Moore's father led. Irons is literally a case of "There but for the Grace of God" goes another black man: behind bars, victim to the prison-industrial complex.

However, Moore's antiracism work has a longer history. Following the police shooting of two black men, Alton Sterling (Baton Rouge, Louisiana) and Philando Castile (Minneapolis) in July 2016, Moore and the other three Lynx co-captains (Seimone Augustus, Lindsay Whalen, and Rebekkah Brunson) wore black t-shirts that read "Change Starts With Us. Justice & Accountability."[4] Together with other her colleagues in the WNBA, Moore has been instrumental in linking professional female athletes to the Say Her Name movement, an organization founded in 2014 to focus attention on female black victims of police violence—such as Michelle Cusseaux (Phoenix) and Kayla Moore (Berkeley, California).[5] (The Say Her Name movement aligns itself with the broader struggle against police brutality but is committed to shining a spotlight on female

3. https://www.thenation.com/article/society/maya-moore-wnba-marriage/.

4. https://www.si.com/wnba/2020/12/23/maya-moore-activism-inspiration-of-the-year-tina-charles.

5. https://www.wgbh.org/news/national-news/2020/07/07/say-her-name-how-the-fight-for-racial-justice-can-be-more-inclusive-of-black-women#:~:text=The%20Say%20Her%20Name%20campaign%2C%20created%20by%20Crenshaw%27s,been%20part%20of%20the%20Black%20Lives%20Matter%20movement.

victims. Hamilton wore his "Breonna Taylor" t-shirt in honor of this movement. Another articulation of this movement has been the campaign to "End White Silence," in which "White Silence" is pronounced—denounced—as "complicity.")

Like the NBA, the WNBA postponed its August 26th and 27th games. This brought renewed attention to the work done by a player such as Angel McCoughtry, a small forward with the Las Vegas Aces. McCoughtry was instrumental in having "Breonna Taylor" inscribed on all WNBA player uniforms. McCoughtry, who attended the University of Louisville, the very city in which Taylor was shot by police, wanted to make sure Taylor's murder remained a focus for the WNBA—as well as, that is, reminding the wider American public of the cost black Americans bear, living as they do in the "most racist country in the world,"[6] "warehoused" as they are in state and federal prisons (many of which are for-profit institutions), without any hope of justice and (largely) devoid of the means to secure a fair trial. Too many of them, especially women such as Cusseaux and Kayla Moore, condemned first to death by police violence and then summarily forgotten.

The NFL Steps Up

In the NFL, the other black majority (again, only in relation to its player personnel) sport in the United States, nine teams, including the Washington franchise, the New York Jets, the Green Bay Packers and the Indianapolis Colts, cancelled their Thursday (August 27) practices in order to address issues of racism and police brutality. Earlier that morning, a former player and currently the league's head of player operations, Troy Vincent, broke down during an interview with ESPN Radio as he reflected on the dangers that his sons, two twenty-somethings and a 15-year-old, face as a matter of daily (black) life.

6. Gina Mizzell, "A W.N.B.A. Veteran Extends Her Influence On and Off the Court," *New York Times,* August 30, 2020.

The shooting of Jacob Blake was simply the latest in a line of difficult issues that made life especially difficult for the NFL in the spring and summer of 2020. A league that is intensely image conscious and that prides itself on executive control, from the commissioner's office (headed by Roger Goodell) to the coaches on the sidelines, spent most of the warmer months of 2020 feeling the heat. Jacob Blake in August 2020 stood then as a bookend to the murder of George Floyd by Derek Chauvin, a white police officer, who held his knee on the neck of George Floyd for nine minutes and twenty-nine seconds (initially presumed to be for eight minutes and forty-six seconds) in Minneapolis. In the wake of this sadistic act of police brutality, the NFL's star players put together an ad that expressly declared the players' support for the Black Lives Matter movement.

Most prominently, the ad headlined Patrick Mahomes, the Kansas City Chiefs quarterback and the league's 2020 MVP, as well as being the NFL's brightest talent. (Mahomes's team, the Kansas City Chiefs, is a name that has itself come under scrutiny for its stereotyping of America's indigenous communities. Especially, that is, after the NFL's Washington franchise dropped its racist moniker, "Redskins," in July 2020. The team did so under pressure from indigenous activists and, it should be noted, when corporate sponsors such as FedEx,[7] Nike, and PepsiCo threatened to withdraw their financial support.) Also featured in the ad were players such as Odell Beckham Jr. (Cleveland Browns' wide receiver), Saquon Barkeley (NY Giants, running back), Michael Thomas (New Orleans Saints, wide receiver), and Deshaun Watson (Houston Texans, quarterback, a player now under scrutiny for alleged sexual harassment).

---

7. FedEx owns the naming rights to Washington's stadium. https://abcnews.go.com/US/washington-redskins-change-years-backlash/story?id=71744369#:~:text=%22July%2013%2C%202020%20is%20now%20a%20historic%20day,in%20a%20statement%20after%20the%20decision%20was%20announced. The Black Lives Matter was also crucial to Washington abandoning its offensive moniker. The team played the 2020 NFL season as the "Washington Football Team." At the time of writing, it still not rebranded itself.

The NFL, a league in which many of the team owners are Trump supporters (Jerry Jones of the Dallas Cowboys, Bob Kraft of the New England Patriots and Woody Johnson of the New York Jets, to name but three), has long been hostile to any form of public protest.

The risk, which we can also understand as the first condition of utopian thinking, is that the caution of subreption must be taken as a matter of good faith. That is, privileging utopia, with its lack of specificity, in its nonprogrammaticity, requires thinking the dissolution of representative democracy without knowing what is intended to take its place. Utopian thinking, then, as a leap of faith.

Utopian thinking as an absolute necessity. Reflecting on the work of Stokely Carmichael and the Black Power movement in the United States, revolutionary Marxist C.L.R. James reminds us of this. "For the Negro people of the US," James writes, "the socialist society is not a hope, *not what we may hope,* but a compelling necessity."[8] What must be recognized in our moment, is that a utopian society is "not a hope, but a compelling necessity."

We begin our thinking in the most general conceptual and foundational terms: a just, equitable society that guarantees all alimentary needs (housing, nutrition, education, healthcare, personal security, and so on), a comity that depends on a fair exchange between labor and reward, that provides for adequate leisure time (sport, in a reorganized form) and individual pursuit (painting, writing music or poetry, and so on) while also expecting communal commitment, broadly understood. Everyone contributes to, say, the upkeep of the community's physical structures; rotation in executing the menial tasks (garbage collection, delivery of mail, etc.), all the while allowing for whatever special talents members of the community possesses. All this as we keep in mind Jameson's model of the universal army in which everyone does their share.

Two struggles, conducted simultaneously, led by two different constituencies, each commanding its own particular set of resources. In

---

8. C. L. R. James, "Black Power," in *The C. L. R. James Reader*, ed. Anna Grimshaw (Cambridge, Mass.: Blackwell, 1992), 374.

anticipation of the second enfolding the first within its (eventual, uto-pian) self. In so doing, we raise the prospect of political relief, support, and possibly even the need to reorient the black athlete's focus (from securing voting rights to campaigning for the superannuation of that very system). The black athlete's struggle will be supplemented by a Leninist imperative.

The project is no longer to, as current capitalist discourse would have, "grow the pie." (A position advocated, metonymically, by the likes of New York Times columnists Nicholas Kristof and Paul Krugman.) That is, capitalism is always the best elixir for all our social woes. More than that, its only solution. Create the conditions under which minority businesses can take root, flourish, and, in so doing, provide "uplift" not only for the entrepreneurial class, but for a broader swathe of structurally bereft, economically underresourced communities.

This is the sort of bastard capitalist logic, one in which Reaganesque rhetoric—"a rising tide lifts all boats"[9]—meets Booker T. Washington self-help—repurposed, of course, so that the rallying cry is no longer "Up from slavery" but capitalist ascension for "all." Known to us as the determination to found and sustain black and minority owned businesses. "Increase minority ownership." "More black-owned busi-nesses." "Support black businesses."[10]

A greater slice of the pie is not the answer.

The nature of the pie is such that it will never be equitably sliced. In fact, nothing about the model and metaphor of the pie is about equity.

LeBron James's stake in Fenway Sports Group, whose holdings include the Boston Red Sox and Liverpool F.C., expands and inten-

---

9. A phrase Reagan lifted from a 1963 speech by John F. Kennedy; a phrase intended to give rhetorical ballast to what would become known, under Lyndon B. Johnson, as the drive to establish the "Great Society."

10. On this matter, Stokely Carmichael is pointed in his critique: "The society we seek to build among black people is not an oppressive capitalist society—for capitalism by its very nature cannot create structures free from exploitation. We are fighting for the redistribution of wealth and for the end of private property inside the United States" (Carmichael, as quoted in C. L. R. James's "Black Power," 374).

sifies LeBron's investment in capital—increases his wealth. And, to shift historic black paradigms radically, LeBron's wealthiness—or the wealthiness of any other minority figure—elevates him to the status of the "Talented . . . Two Percent?"

It does nothing to reimagine how we might be in the world.

The problem is not that there are too few black billionaires. The problem is that there are billionaires at all.

Let us address that problem by disposing of the logic of the pie entirely.

Chris Rock, a black man of no small means, understands the logic of wealth and how it perpetuates itself im-perfectly.

As encapsulated in a Chris Rock joke. A little dated, but, indulge me: "What's the difference between Shaq and the guy who signs his checks?"

"Shaq is rich. The guy who signs his checks . . . that guy is wealthy."

Wealth is the product of capital accumulated over generations. "Rich" as LeBron might be, the best he can hope for is that his grandchildren will be wealthy. (Jordan, for his part, is well on the way to being wealthy, part owner of an NBA franchise, among his other assets and investments.) Wealth, largely the product of "unearned"—"smart investments," "smart investment strategies"—capital (or, capital reproducing itself without labor), is the history of capital accumulation.

To phrase the matter crudely. Riches can be enjoyed, shared, even. Wealth is inherited. Wealth in itself inscribes the history of capital accumulation. And wealth can only be accumulated through exploitation.

And the ability to exploit is not bound to race.

It is driven by the desire for capital accumulation.

In Chris Rock's terms, it is Shaq's or LeBron's or Chris Paul's ambition to turn the economic tables and, instead of cashing the checks he is given (which makes him richer), he becomes the one who "signs the checks." The surest sign of his having become wealthy.

Michael Jordan signs checks.

9. Colin Kaepernick

THE NFL'S OPPOSITION to protest was, of course, made tangible when Colin Kaepernick, then the quarterback for the San Francisco 49ers, took a knee to bring awareness to police brutality against minority communities in America. Beginning in August 2016, Kaepernick's action was supported by a (relatively) small number of other players. Among them were his 49ers teammate Eric Reid; Brandon Marshall of the Denver Broncos ("I'm against social injustice");[1] Jurrell Casey, Wesley Woodyard, and Jason McCourty of the Tennessee Titans; Martellus Bennett and Devin McCourty (Jason's twin brother) of the New England Patriots; Marcus Peters of the Kansas City Chiefs; and the entire player roster and coaching staff of the Seattle Seahawks. Kaepernick's action, another moment of resistance through stillness (the black body publicly withholding itself in an act of disobedience, the refusal to act in accordance with the demands of the hegemonic order),[2] caused considerable controversy, not the least of which was a clearly oppositional stance taken by Goodell and the league office. Then in the final year of his contract with the 49ers, Kaepernick found himself punished for his actions. Despite his obvious talent, including having led the 49ers to

---

1. https://www.foxsports.com/nfl/gallery/athletes-who-have-joined-colin-kaepernick-s-national-anthem-protest-091216.
2. This is precisely the issue I take up in *In Motion, at Rest: The Event of the Athletic Body* (Minneapolis: University of Minnesota Press, 2013).

the Super Bowl in 2011, when they lost, narrowly, to the Baltimore Ravens, no team would sign Kaepernick because he was steadfast in his determination to take a knee during the national anthem.

Kaepernick has not played in the NFL since.

Kaepernick, although not mentioned, is the presence that haunts the 2020 NFL players' ad. Confronted with a nation grappling with systemic racism, Goodell apologized, within some 24 hours, for "not having listened to the players'" previous grievances. The year 2016, and Kaepernick, were clearly on Goodell's mind. Henceforth, kneeling for the national anthem was permitted. Out of the "canceling," to use the current terminology, of Kaepernick, and the death of George Floyd, the (constitutional) right to protest police brutality was won.

Chalk up another win for reformism.

Meanwhile, Kaepernick remains unemployed. A powerful catalyst who, much like Muhammad Ali in 1967 when he refused the draft, brought attention to an issue that, in truth, has for too long been an unarguable fact of black life in America.

Three Ironies

The biracial Colin Kaepernick, born to a white mother (Heidi Russo) and an African American father (who separated from his mother before Kaepernick was born), was adopted and raised by white parents, Rick and Teresa Kaepernick. Born in, as historical irony would have it, Milwaukee, Wisconsin, Kaepernick was raised in Fond du Lac, Wisconsin, before his family moved to California. Kaepernick excelled at baseball, basketball, and football in Turlock, CA.

In our moment, all things involving police brutality and the black athlete lead back to Colin Kaepernick. But history had one more coincidence to offer. George Hill's decision came about forty-eight hours before the fifty-seventh anniversary of the March on Washington. On that monumental occasion in August 1963, in that "I Have A Dream" address, Martin Luther King Jr. twice makes mention of excessive police force unjustly trained on black bodies.

He condemns those who make the "Negro" a "victim of the unspeakable horrors of police brutality," leaving black bodies "staggered by the winds of police brutality."[3]

Martin Luther King's dream is Colin Kaepernick's dream is George Hill's dream. A dream now, at the very least, thrice unrealized; a dream crushed by police batons, attacked by Bull Connor's dogs, killed by a policeman's unmovable knee, maimed by seven bullets. And, because of it, turmoil will ensue: "There will be neither rest nor tranquility in America until the Negro is granted his citizenship rights. The whirlwinds of revolt will continue to shake the foundations of our nation until the bright day of justice emerges."[4] For a moment the epicenter of that "whirlwind" was Kenosha, Wisconsin, as it was in Minneapolis three short months prior. We can only guess where it will be headquartered next.

The question, however, remains: How profoundly must the "foundations of our nation" be shaken, how many more black lives must be sacrificed to police brutality, how much more black, Latino, native American, Asian, and yes, white, poverty must be experienced, how many more times must black and minority lives be shown to be most vulnerable to health crises, Covid-19 being merely the latest iteration of this phenomenon, before the "bright day of justice emerges"? When is enough truly, and finally, Enough? Metonymically, Danny Green and Amir Coffey would like to know. How much more? How many more, Zubica, Mason, and Wannamaker would like to know? Can "Enough" be quantified? And, if so, can it be done with any arithmetical precision? What will the final tally be?

Enough as that moment when the questions that the black athlete provokes demands such a reckoning that the constitutive limits of the players' struggle is apprehended as that juncture where the black athlete must reach outside of itself to find an answer. Only then can

3. Martin Luther King Jr., *I Have a Dream: Writings & Speeches That Changed the World,* ed. James Melvin Washington (New York: Harper One, 1992), 104.

4. King Jr., 103.

what is at stake be fully addressed. It is not enough to campaign for reform. It is only, paradoxically, through a complete reorganization of society that the black athlete—that all athletes—is released into the freedom to simply play. When it will no longer be necessary for a black athlete to save us.

To declare, then, that only a black athlete can save us now, is to speak out of firm historical grounding. It is also, however, to recognize how the various discourses that constitute the black radical tradition reinforce, coincide with, and support each other. And sometimes, it is hoped, contradict each other to the point of superannuation. It is to draw a line, sometimes direct, but more often jagged and winding, that links a historic speech (King) with a determination to withhold black labor (Hill). It is to understand that black eloquence, black anger, and black silence belong, no matter their distinction, to the same political—and, yes, ethical—register. No matter that he may forswear it, and we have no reason to believe he would, George Hill, like Martin Luther King, dreams of what is not. An America that can live, in good faith, in good conscience, if you insist, with itself. Of what must be. Justice. Of what must not be. Continuing injustice. Police brutality.

Colin Kaepernick took a knee and then, it turns out, it was another knee—of an entirely more violent nature—that made the NFL commissioner to publicly speak to the reality of police brutality against black bodies. Kaepernick's knee found its fatal corollary in Derek Chauvin's knee. Kaepernick's (taking a) knee inflicted no physical harm on anyone. Chauvin's killed a black man. Kaepernick's (taking a knee) provoked outrage amongst white nationalists, white "patriots" (the American national anthem is sacred, stand for it or be condemned; condemned as what exactly one is, which is probably wise not to probe too deeply), a racist white president (Trump), and all their echo chambers in the right-wing media. For at least a moment, Chauvin's knee promised to bring, if not a nation, then all those with the potential to be (right) thinking human beings—that is, those with even a modicum of decency and the smallest appetite for justice—to its senses. The death effected by Chauvin's knee, which has never been joined in conversation to Kaepernick's, opened the door—briefly, just wedging the door ajar ever so slightly—to the possibility of a nation willing to take up the work of racial reckoning.

Taking a Knee, Keeping a Knee on a Black Man's Neck

Amidst all the violence, amidst the myriad protests that wracked and continue to wrack, this nation, Kaepernick maintained a steadfast silence. No one would identify Kaepernick as an oracle. There was no need to. What Kaepernick took a knee for would not be recognized, by a large swathe of white America, for what it is: the fundamental "common sense" of the America political—the right to peaceful protest.

The logic that governs white America's relationship to the black body is always, a priori, based on the presumption of black criminality. Contained within that logic, as we well know, is the all-too accepted "need" for excessive police force in relation to the black body (no-knock warrants, tasing, all the force it takes to subdue the black body, and, of course, the use of deadly force). This is the path that leads to black death and the need for large-scale black incarceration.

Kaepernick's was a historically informed, politically critical, taking of the knee. The NFL, the Trump White House, the rabid white nationalists in the conservative media, white Republicans, and their fellow-travelers all across America (I do not doubt that more than a few Democrats were similarly ill-disposed to Kaepernick's protest), glued to their TV screens on Sunday to watch the NFL, declared themselves virulently opposed to taking a knee.

Derek Chauvin's knee, on the other hand, has thrown the entire nation into a cataclysm of . . . violence, protests, utopian occupation (Seattle), counterprotests (Portland) . . . with more in the offing. America, the Land of, the Land with, a Wounded Knee. (A nation *Wounded,* as in Percival Everett's novel of the same name; a nation where, in the white West, not far from Laramie, Wyoming, an indigenous ranch owner finds *"Red Nigger"*[5] written in the snow, written with the blood of his dead cattle. The only person with whom the indigenous rancher can share the inscription with is his black neighbor.) One man's kneeling is another man's deadly force. A white man's knee is a black man's death. A black man's kneeling on an NFL sideline prefigures a black man's death by kneeling by a white police officer on a black man's neck.

5. Percival Everett, *Wounded* (St. Paul, Minn.: Graywolf Press, 2005), 111, emphasis in original.

10. Silence Reverberates

ON AUGUST 26, 2020, George Hill joined a lineage that runs from the fin de siècle boxer Jack Johnson, the first black heavyweight champion, through Althea Gibson, the first black woman to win a tennis Grand Slam tournament, to the iconic heavyweight boxer Muhammad Ali, the first athlete to declare himself "G.O.A.T." (the greatest of all time), to Olympic athletes John Carlos and Tommy Smith, remembered and revered now for the defiant black power salute they offered in 1968 on the podium in Mexico City. As we just discussed, this lineage reached a more modest, but no less resonant, articulation in the contemporary with Kaepernick's taking a knee.

And now, once more, we are made to see how black athletes understand themselves compelled to act because of what is not. Once more, like 1968, ours is another "sweltering summer of the Negro's legitimate discontent," and this "mood"—in Heidegger's sense, an attunement that emerges out of a specific milieu—"will not pass until there is an invigorating autumn of freedom and equality."[1] In the bubble, there above their numbers, where their names used to be, one could now read "Black Lives Matter," "Say Her Name," "Enough," "Vote," and, yes, "Freedom" and "Equality."

It remains doubtful, however, as white nationalists streamed into Portland, Oregon, to attack antipolice brutality and antifascist

---

1. King Jr., *I Have a Dream*, 103.

protesters, that the "autumn" that followed the racist police violence of the 2020 spring-summer will lead to "freedom and equality." In what kind of a world is the work of antifascists, abbreviated, to inflect the term with an ominousness that is not native to it, to "Antifa," a political pejorative? In America. Only in America. To oppose fascism is to render the antifascist self a criminal.

Within such an environment it is no wonder that any poetic turn, if such an inclination can be mustered, tends, rather, toward the tragically Shakespearean. Specifically, we invoke *Richard III*: "Now is the winter of our discontent." About which, contra Gloucester, there can be made nothing "glorious." About which it must be said that much of the history of black life in the United States has been nothing but one long "winter of discontent." Or, an all-too brief spring followed by one more long winter. A long winter that is, under the worst possible circumstances, only broken up by those black athletes who can birth, once again, a tenuous interlude—or, in Antonio Gramsci's more hopeful nomenklatura, an interregnum—that throws off the oppressive veil of winter.

In his work on forgiveness, Vladimir Jankélévitch offers an insight that is pertinent to the repetition of responsibility that falls to those who have to effect change under the most arduous conditions. Those who have the courage, the will, and those who can seize the opportunity as it—sometimes entirely unexpectedly, carpe diem—presents itself to them, to start again. As if for the first time, in Jacques Derrida's terms.

Framing his argument in terms of "moral progress," Jankélévitch writes: "Moral progress advances only by the deliberate effort of a decision that is intermittent and spasmodic and in the tension of an indefatigable starting-over."[2] "Intermittent" is to acknowledge that the actions taken and the burdens endured by Jack Johnson—hunted by police across state lines, for the sin of insisting on his

---

2. Vladimir Jankélévitch, *Forgiveness,* trans. Andrew Kelley (Chicago: University of Chicago Press, 2013), 42.

right to marry white women—made it imperative for white America to institute a chasm between Johnson and his black successor, Joe Louis. Johnson's blatant disregard for America's racist norms, his flouting of white conventions, explains the political straightjacket imposed on Louis. Under no circumstances would the second black heavyweight champion of the world, known as the "Brown Bomber," be allowed to follow in the footsteps of his Galveston, Texas, predecessor, "Papa Jack." Aggressive, self-confident blackness, Johnson, was transformed—muted—into black quiescence, Louis. For white America, the black boxer has no political use—or personhood—outside of the ring.

It is also to recognize the "deliberate effort" expended by black women in world tennis to achieve a "merely" "spasmodic" result—that is, the sudden, brief, sporadic, presence of black women in the world's most "lilywhite" game. In 1956 Althea Gibson became the first black woman to win a tennis major when she triumphed at the French Open. Gibson went on to win both Wimbledon and the U.S. Nationals (what we now know as the U.S. Open) in 1957 and 1958. Gibson's successes notwithstanding, her career must have been a time of isolation, the loneliness and a consciousness of a world-crushing singularity for her. Every season must have felt like an "indefatigable starting-over." How similar must this sense of isolation have been for Zina Garrison, who starred in tennis in the 1980s through the 1990s. Garrison was not as successful as Gibson, although she did reach a highest ranking of number four in the world, in addition to winning three mixed doubles Grand Slam titles, but she was made fully aware of her relationship to Gibson. Based exclusively on her race, Garrison was dubbed the "new Althea Gibson."[3]

Garrison's racially overdetermined, superimposed relationship to Gibson must have been its own onerous burden. It was also, however, a "tension-filled" "starting-over." Garrison, unlike her white

---

3. https://www.theguardian.com/sport/2006/may/07/tennis.features.

contemporaries, such as, say, Chrissy Evert and Martina Navratilova, did not only have to attend to the weight of her own professional ambitions and expectations, she was also made acutely aware of her racial singularity. Every match, every Grand Slam major, must have had made Garrison feel that every time she stepped onto the court, once more, "moral progress begins from zero. There is no other ethical *continuity* than this exhausting *continuation* of 're-launch' and resumption."[4] Garrison, like Gibson before her, had to begin again—from point "zero." As if for the first time. Singularity, the exceptional black athlete, is an unrelenting, ever-self-renewing burden, to be taken up every time the black athlete takes, in Gibson's and Garrison's cases, the court. "Relaunch," once more. An "exhausting" business. Physically wearying, ontologically exhausting. How many times must the black athlete begin again because he or she is deprived of, is denied, a genealogical "continuity" that is not so overwhelmed by the lack of an easy chronological "continuity"?

4. https://www.theguardian.com/sport/2006/may/07/tennis.features.

11. The Peculiar Science of Black Athletic Entropy

TO BE A BLACK ATHLETE who takes up the political cudgels in her or his moment is to live, after a fashion, an entropic life. In Jankélévitch's terms, it is to commit, unknowingly and yet assuredly, to conducting a political struggle. This does not mean that every generation of black athletes will be called upon to speak against racism. It means, rather, that every generation of black athletes—as a collectivity, as a singular figure—must live in expectation of such a demand. It is also to know that the more protracted the discontinuity, the more difficult and challenging it will be to establish, if only for a moment, a reconnection to what-was, and thereby to renew continuity. It is to know how onerous it will be to mark, if only barely, its own distinction. To interpose the black athlete between racist sociopolitical realities and the position of relative possibility—a place from which to articulate against, to speak for—allows it to draw on the previous continuity. It will, however, never quite seem as if every act of resistance, of speaking against, has not been created anew. Yet again. The peculiar science of black athletic entropy is such that the black athlete's political resources always seem on the verge of depletion. Because even when the long discontinuity provides the chance for replenishment, the resources to hand never seem to rise above the level of what is absolutely necessary. And sometimes, by which one means "all too often," there is less on hand than what is needed. *This is how the art of making-do and the technique of digging deep is renewed.*

Jankélévitch understands this political demand as relentless. The black athlete knows, as a matter of course, that the road ahead will always be marked by the repeated need for "an indefatigable starting-over." To secure even the smallest gain, the black athlete must be inexhaustible in her political commitment. There can be, if not from one moment to the next, then certainly from epoch to the next, no respite, no letting up. (In the NBA, it can be argued that there was less expected from Michael Jordan and the Dream Team generation than has been the case for the likes of current superstars such as LeBron James, the inscrutable Kawhi Leonard, and the sweet-shooting Steph Curry).

However, what must not be lost sight of is that "indefatigability" is, before itself, a recognition of the capacity of the black athlete to "start over." The reserves of energy, political commitment, sheer will, and the unending—if the term is understood episodically rather than literally—determination to return, Sisyphus-like, to the scene of the crime to take up the battle anew. To take up the cudgels again, the foreboding odds against the black athlete notwithstanding.

It is, as it were, to at once stand on the shoulders of Gibson, Ali, Carlos and Smith, and Arthur Ashe, and to know that sometimes all that is to be gained from such a historic invocation is the name itself, the memory of the name, and, as such, the name as a potential point of political convergence, and solace or hope, at best. It is also to accept that all the remaining energy—because, we can agree, no political movement has ever been, or will ever be, fueled by an inexhaustible supply of energy—must draw from the future as well as the past.

No wonder that Jameson declares revolution the work of the young.

Sometimes it is, literally, a matter of gathering what is to hand—the moment, a reserve of energy that is running low, a formidable adversary, an entirely unsympathetic racial climate—and struggling with those resources.

Even Sisyphus, for all his courage, allowed his shoulders to droop. Just now and then. In the hope, of course, that replenishment would emerge from one place or, if not that one, perhaps another.

It is to choose Sisyphus's capacity—enforced, one acknowledges—for dogged return over respite. Even, that is, as we acknowledge Ella Baker's own brand of dogged determination that is lodged in her clarion call for persistent struggle: "We who love freedom cannot rest." Baker, who worked in the Civil Rights Movement for some five decades, all of it away from the spotlight, was her own brand of "indefatigability."

However, the logic of entropy, as offered here, is based precisely in the need to know that "rest" is that political stillness—stillness, at-restness, not quiescence or quietude—which can be imposed from without, which imposes its own rules, which follows its own schedule. (That is to say nothing of the restorative qualities of "rest." It is to know "rest" as the condition, spoken or unarticulated, that sustains "indefatigability.")

It is not so much that entropy and "indefatigability" stand opposed to one another. It is rather that they are, if the contradiction can be understood as a matter of political timing, complementary.

Every moment, as we well know, is prone to exhaustion. Every moment, however, is also entirely capable of replenishing itself. If not in that exact moment, then certainly soon enough to summon up all that is needed—or, sometimes maybe just a little less or even a little more—in that conjuncture.

As Paul Simon phrases it in, appropriately, "Boy in the Bubble," "It's everybody jumpstart / Every generation throws a hero up the pop charts."[1] *Sometimes it's the journeyman shooting guard, the guy who can makes threes but is not going to make the All-Star team, that gives you the "jumpstart." He gives you just what you need. Doing that makes him the "hero." You never know who the "pop charts" is going to "throw up."*

Sometimes the "hero" is just the solid professional with a racial conscience. Sometimes it's just the guy who has had enough. The

1. https://www.paulsimon.com/track/the-boy-in-the-bubble-6/.

journeyman who says, simultaneously, "No más" and, in the spirit of Cesar Chavez and the United Farm Workers, "Sí, se puede."

"Enough," itself a tired cry, a cry wrought out of exhaustion, "I have had enough of this." (Or, "We have had enough of this brutality.") Sometime such a cry is sufficient to produce the courage demanded by the moment.

Sometimes George Hill is the form that generational responsibility assumes.

Being able to rely on this, that is what emanates most loudly from Cornel West's plaintive, worn out by death, gratitude to his "brothers in the NBA." It is always good to know that as a black person you can count on someone other than yourself. Too often black people are left out on their own, left to their own devices, made to rely on their historically depleted resources.

Arthur Ashe felt this acutely as he made his way from the segregated courts of his native Richmond, Virginia, to the manicured lawns of Wimbledon.

In his first lonely years in MLB, as we know from Roger Kahn's magnificent love letter to the Brooklyn Dodgers, *The Boys of Summer,* and from the many biographies and histories on Jackie Robinson, as we know from his widow Rachel Robinson's testimonies, Jackie Robinson's singularity was something on the order of a crushing burden. We know this from Lewis Hamilton's several public addresses on the issue before and during the 2020 Formula I (FI). The only black driver in FI, Hamilton called the 2020 season, which he has dedicated to the Black Lives Matter movement, a "lonely journey,"[2] a fact that he attributes only partly to the absence of crowds at the various FI circuits because of Covid-19. As he successfully chased a record-tying seventh championship (which tied him with Michael Schumacher) and as he streaked past Schumacher's record of ninety-one Grand Prix wins (at the time of writing, Hamilton has won an unprecedented ninety-nine races), Hamilton was also

2. https://www.theguardian.com/sport/2020/aug/17/lewis-hamilton-says-pursuing-the-2020-f1-title-has-been-a-lonely-journey.

in the forefront of compelling FI to speak to racial injustices and to diversify a sport that is, and has been until Hamilton's emergence, overwhelmingly white. (Hamilton's efforts have included getting drivers to take a knee before every Grand Prix. Most, if not all, of his fellow-drivers have done so, a testament to Hamilton's standing among his peers.) The effect of such a "lonely journey" clearly weighs on Hamilton, even as he continues to dominate the sport like no other FI driver before him.

Like Hamilton, NASCAR's Darrell "Bubba" Wallace Jr. finds himself the racial outlier in a historically white sport, backed by an overwhelmingly white fan base (80 percent white, 37 percent of whom are southerners)[3] who—until June 2020—seemed to wave the Confederate flag[4] and other such racist paraphernalia with gusto, and without any self-reflection. (In fact, many threatened to boycott NASCAR once the organization took the decision to ban Old Glory.) It took Wallace's declamation of racism, his decision to wear a shirt that read "I Can't Breathe" (a critique of police brutality), backed by the "Black Lives Matter" decal he displayed on his car, to bring attention to the matter. (Wallace has, in his most difficult moments, found support from both inside and outside of NASCAR. Seven-time NASCAR champion Jimmie Johnson, white, sent a message of encouragement via social media, as did the likes of LeBron James and Chelsea Clinton.)[5] And, to effect action, once more it falls to the black athlete to initiate the discussion, to lead the movement, and to ensure that change, no matter how minimal or superficial, takes place.

Reformism is a lonely business.

3. https://www.rawstory.com/2020/06/nascar-fans-explode-with-anger-over-confederate-flag-ban-good-luck-on-filling-those-stands/.

4. https://www.cnn.com/2020/06/10/us/nascar-bans-confederate-flag-spt-trnd/index.html.

5. https://www.dailymail.co.uk/news/article-8503171/Bubba-Wallaces-mom-told-ignore-Trumps-noose-apology-demand-fix-stupid.html. Wallace's mother, Desiree Wallace, offered a sharp retort to Trump when he attacked her son: "You can't fix stupid," Mrs. Wallace informed her son.

Wallace's success in highlighting NASCAR's racism is especially noteworthy because, in 2015, a white man, Dylan Roof, walked into a Bible study meeting at the Emanuel Methodist Episcopal Church in Charleston, South Carolina, and murdered nine black people who had welcomed him into their midst. Urged by some in its ranks, most notably, Dale Earnhardt Jr., a star in his own right and the son of the legendary Dale Earnhardt Sr., to ban the Confederate flag at its meetings, NASCAR made a half-hearted attempt.[6] This after the Confederate flag was taken down at the South Carolina State Capitol, but Old Glory remained part of NASCAR's culture, its adherents declaring themselves loyal to their Southern heritage. Earnhardt Jr. was of a different opinion: "It belongs in the history books and that's about it."

Wallace and Hamilton are both the sons of racially mixed parentage. Wallace's father is white and his mother is African American. Hamilton's father is black (of Caribbean origin) and his mother is a white Englishwoman. Aside from their singular status within their motor sports, they do not have much in common. Hamilton, prior to the pandemic, enjoyed a jet set, cosmopolitan lifestyle. The Englishman hobnobs with movie stars—Hamilton dedicated his 2020 Belgian Grand Prix (GP) victory to Chadwick Boseman, who died that weekend. He pals around with fashion moguls (he took a day off to attend Karl Lagerfeld's funeral). His ex-girlfriend is a pop star. Hollywood types, that's where Hamilton is to be found. He dominates a sport that is increasingly international in its reach, with GPs in China, Azerbaijan, Bahrain, Brazil, to say nothing of the European, Asian and rest of the North American circuit.

NASCAR, with its Southern (U.S.) roots (some of which can be traced to a bootlegging past), is a fiercely nationalist motor sport. No traipsing around the world, no race in Japan followed by one in Malaysia. No, one Sunday its Darlington in South Carolina and

6. https://www.washingtonpost.com/nation/2020/06/11/nascar-confederate-flag-2015/.

the next Talladega Superspeedway in Alabama followed by a race at Martinsville Speedway in Virginia. Even Wallace's very moniker, "Bubba" (often understood as a reference to a white southerner), would make him seem of a piece with NASCAR. Of which he isn't, at least not completely. And much of this has to do with the motor sport in which he races. Unlike Hamilton, seven-time FI champion, Wallace is not the top performer in NASCAR. An ocean (in truth, oceans, given FI's global reach) separates the two black racers.

They are linked, however, by being the only one in their sport.

It is for this reason that Hamilton's sober reflections remind us, if reminding were needed, of the price that Serena Williams has had to pay for her outspokenness. Williams has won twenty-three Grand Slam titles—comprising the four major tournaments: the Australian, French, and U.S. Opens, as well as Wimbledon. Only the Australian Margaret Court, with twenty-four, has won more. Like Billie Jean King, Martina Navratilova, Chris Evert, and Steffi Graff before her, Williams—more commonly referred to simply as "Serena"—has re-defined the game. With her power (her serve and her ground strokes are formidable), her strength, her speed and agility, combined with a fierce determination, Serena has dominated women's tennis for much of the last two decades. If King gained fame not only for her game but also for advocacy for women's tennis, and Navratilova became a champion for gay women players, then Serena's burden has been—as much, if not more than her predecessors'—singular. While earlier black women's players, most notably, as we said, Althea Gibson, were pathbreaking in their accomplishments as it pertained to race and racism, they were not as aggressive, public, and outspoken in their critiques of racism in the women's game or of racism as the lived reality of black people in America. Serena has forged her own way. Bold, unrepentant, and the dominant player of her era to boot, Serena has completely reconceived the way in which tennis can be played and, as importantly, she has laid down her marker as a proud black woman champion.

In Serena's case, only the funkiness of James Brown will do: "Say it loud / I'm black and I'm proud."

And for this she has paid a price, singled out for critiques and sometimes even for her game. As if that were not enough, in addition to being critiqued for speaking in favor of social justice, Serena has had to endure the denigration of the black (female) body. On at least one occasion, Serena was ridiculed by the white Belgian player Kim Clijsters.[7] Before one match against Williams, Klijsters stuffed towels into her shirt and skirt to mock Serena's physique. Whether or not she was aware of it, Klijsters was evoking the "Hottentot Venus" imagery that has been used to demean black women since the 19th century, at least. All the while, as she was doing this, Klijsters smiled, smug and self-satisfied. Indifferent to the racist stereotypes she was summoning to life, once more. As if this were her first time with the joke. As if it were now her turn to indict the black body. And to laugh while doing it.

However, as Serena's career enters its twilight years, Williams finds herself surrounded by a new generation of black women tennis players. The most notable among this new generation are Coco Gauff, Madison Keyes, Sloane Stephens, and Taylor Townsend, the last of whom is less well known the others. By some measure, the most prominent among this generation, and the player who seems most likely to dominate the game in the next few years, is Naomi Osaka. Born in Japan to a Haitian father and a Japanese mother, Osaka has lived in the United States since the age of 3. (Osaka has spoken forcefully about the racist challenges she has faced, and continues to face, as a black Japanese woman in Japanese society. For Osaka this is a critical issue since she plays under the Japanese flag. Osaka has spoken about race/racism in Japan and the ways in which the late-L.A. Lakers star Kobe Bryant,[8] who was named after

7. See Claudia Rankine's mediation on the Williams-Clijsters encounter in *Citizen: An American Lyric* (Minneapolis: Graywolf Press, 2014).

8. Bryant cemented his relationship to Kobe, Japan, when he donated toward the city's relief fund in the wake of the 1995 earthquake that the city suffered. Bryant was named "Kobe" because his father had a taste for Kobe beef.

the famous Kobe beef, mentored her.)[9] Among the black women of her generation on the international tennis circuit, Osaka has been the most outspoken on racism.[10] On the evening of August 26, Osaka announced that she would not play her scheduled semifinal match at the Western & Southern Open. Osaka had intended to quit the tourney, but she agreed to continue in the event after play was canceled on August 27.

Taking a different, but nevertheless complementary, tack during the 2020 U.S. Open, Osaka wore at least five distinct black facemasks during the tournament. Across each of the facemasks emblazoned, in white, was a name: Breonna Taylor, Ahmaud Arbery, Elijah McClain, Trayvon Martin, and George Floyd. Because of the popularity of tennis, and because she is the presumed heir to Serena Williams's throne, Osaka has pronounced it her responsibility to keep the reality of police brutality in the forefront of the sport's consciousness.[11]

The discontinuity, the path that leads from Venus and Serena Williams to the Osakas and the Gauffs, is abbreviated. The distance between them shorter. Consequently, there is—in this instance—less need for an absolute "relaunch." In this case, it would seem, it is not really necessary to "start over." At least not as we knew it in its past incarnations. Sometimes the logic of entropy is insufficient to the exigencies—the eruption of life into pure political possibility—of the moment. Sometimes, as in the case of Osaka, the effect of "indefatigability" is such that there is no real need to "start over." Sometimes, after the briefest of pauses, things simply keep going. Sometimes it is "continuity" that holds sway, and one movement, moment, one iconic or even unexceptional figure, mutates into the

9. https://www.theguardian.com/sport/2020/aug/25/naomi-osaka-reflects-on-challenges-of-being-black-and-japanese.

10. In addition to, as we have seen, her determination to speak out about mental health, which she did, painfully, in announcing her decision to withdraw from Wimbledon 2021.

11. https://www.theguardian.com/sport/2020/sep/09/naomi-osaka-victims-racial-injustice-us-open-masks-tennis-george-floyd.

next. Sometimes the handing off, or over, of political responsibility, from one generation to the next, is barely detectable. Differently phrased, it becomes discernible only as we find ourselves turning today to this figure, rather than that one, the one we relied upon just yesterday. Or maybe it just seems that way.

As importantly, and here the political emergence of George Hill offers itself as an object lesson, in some instances a journeyman (professional)—a decent but not exceptional—athlete will do just as well as an icon.

The NBA, we can say, may be not only the most progressive force in American politics, it may also be the force with the deepest bench, so to speak. At the very least, it possesses the political bench from which, seemingly, any—one dare not say "even" in this context, such is Hill's signality—backup (point guard) can emerge as the player most appropriate for the hour. Cometh the hour, cometh a George Hill.

12. The Burden of Over-Representation, Curiously Borne by Woods and Jordan

THIS DISCOURSE, on the exacting cost of bearing the burden of over-representation, gives one pause when considering Tiger Woods's position on the PGA (Professional Golfers' Association) tour. When Woods arrived on the scene in the mid- to late 1990s, already a player of whom much was expected after a magnificent college career (Stanford University), he became the first black golfer who promised to win a Major. With his 1997 victory, Woods became the youngest player ever to win a Major, and, into the bargain, he won by twelve strokes, the biggest margin of victory at Augusta.

Woods has, of course, since his first triumph at the Masters tournament at Augusta, Georgia, in 1997, gone on to win fifteen Majors, putting him second only to Jack Nicklaus's eighteen.

When Woods won at Augusta in 1997, he explicitly thanked Charlie Sifford and Calvin Peete, the pioneering black golfers who had preceded him on the PGA tour. (Woods's son is named Charlie. Whether or not it is honor of Sifford, I can only speculate. Suffice it to say that in August 2020, Charlie Axel Woods was the runaway at the U.S. Kids golf event in Florida.)[1] In 1957 Sifford, in a field

1. https://www.today.com/parents/tiger-woods-caddies-his-11-year-old-son-charlie-u-t189653.

that included white golfers, won the Long Beach Open, making him the first black player to win a PGA event. The Detroit native Peete won 12 events on tour, making him the most successful black golfer prior to Woods.

There was little continuity between Sifford and Peete, and maybe even less between Peete and Woods. In fact, Woods's iconic status in golf may, for reasons that are both rooted in race and professional accomplishment, be utterly distinct from it. Logic—status, accomplishments—determines that. The second most successful golfer in the history of the game is closest only to the player ahead of him, as it should be.

Woods is thus discontinuous, but his singularity derives from an entirely different source.

However, Woods is also discontinuous, at least in relation to, say, LeBron James, more or less a contemporary, in that he is not a black athlete who has a record of speaking out on matters of social justice.

Neither, however, one hastens to add, is Woods quite of a piece with Michael Jordan, who infamously declared himself indentured to capital before all else. A native of Wilmington, North Carolina, Jordan was asked to support a black Democratic senatorial candidate, Harvey Gantt, the mayor of Charlotte. In that 1990 race, Gantt was running against the incumbent senator, Jesse Helms, an avowed segregationist. Jordan would not do so, although he did send the Gantt campaign a check. Jordan's logic was governed by economic considerations: "Republicans buy sneakers too." How does one negate such an irrefutable logic? Nike's main pitch man was true to his pocketbook. (It should be added that this is not an apocryphal story. Jordan admits as much in *The Last Dance,* a quite remarkable ESPN documentary on his Chicago Bulls. Jordan was politically indicted for his nonendorsement by many in the African American community, a decision that has cast something of a shadow over him ever since.)[2]

2. *The Last Dance* does, however, show Jordan to be a figure of some complexity. Admiring of Ali and his activism, Jordan did not seek to inherit the role of the black activist-athlete. More than anything, what *The Last*

Discontinuity assumes many iterations, all of them, in their own way, different. Thus the curious—and intriguing—case of Eldrick "Tiger" Woods.

Still, as the son of an African American father and a Thai mother (Woods's preferred self-designation is a neologism, "Cablanasian." It is composite term, knitted together out of Caucasian, black, Native American, and Asian, so as to give equal credence to his African American, Asian, and indigenous heritage), as a trailblazing black golfer, as a black golfer who has been on the receiving end of racism: one wonders about what kind of loneliness, what mode of apartness, has beset Woods in the course of his career.

Dance brings home is Jordan's intensity and competitiveness, not only as an athlete but as a human being. Every engagement, from playing cards for high stakes on the team bus to playing golf, was for Jordan—is for Jordan— an opportunity to test himself against others. Most refreshing about the documentary, however, is Jordan's willingness to let loose, to spew invective—he is not reluctant to use the expletive, a former Detroit Pistons guard is memorably on the receiving end of one such barrage—as easily as he gives voice to his deep affection and respect for his most loyal teammate, Scottie Pippen.

13. Change Is Everywhere, or So It Seems

WHEN THE NFL PLAYERS RELEASED THEIR AD, I was surprised to see the New York Giants' Saquon Barkley as part of the lineup. I am a New York Giants fan, and I can attest, sadly, that this is a staid and conservative franchise. "Buttoned-up," "straitlaced," "by the book," as aesthetically exciting as a Brooks Brothers suit, that is how I understand the Giants. Proudly blue collar is how less jaundiced fans see "Big Blue." However, even my sclerotic (hardened by tradition gone stale) Giants have found themselves unable to resist the winds of change. Amidst the broader socioeconomic concerns, a pandemic that threatens the health and safety of the players and their families (to say nothing of the broader community), and the prospect of playing before empty stands, with players almost certain to take a knee during the playing of the national anthem to protest police brutality, Barkley, the Giants' star running back, expressly raised the possibility of the team sitting out a game in protest. In the aftermath of the George Floyd killing, Barkley was the Giants player featured in an ad that spoke out against racism and in favor of the Black Lives Matter movement. As a black Giants fan, it is beginning to feel a little like "Big Blue" has caught up, finally, to the 1960s.

It proved to be a tense summer, Ezra. Michelle Obama reminded us of it when she named our condition "systemic racism."[1] We are living in a country that feels as though it is on the precipice of some great disaster. Foreboding is everywhere. Despite this, a significant swathe of white America remains, at best, indifferent to black death, at worst, willing to stand by, tacitly supporting this violence. A tacit support that calls, from Trump in his time at 1600 Pennsylvania Avenue on down, loudly, for "law and order." No doubt, my son, you're savvy enough to know that such rhetoric amounts to the countenancing of more black death. By local police officers or the federal reinforcements called in to restore "law and order."

Sometimes, as in Minneapolis, Portland, and Kenosha, things take an even more ominous turn. White vigilantes, both local and from out of state, either instigate or heed, sometimes it's the same thing, the call to protect "property."

In the name of "property" all kinds of violence against bodies—black, white, Asian, indigenous, Latina/o—protesting police brutality can be called into being. We saw this in Minneapolis, where a fascist white actor instigated violence, only to have the legitimately peaceful protesters impugned. Even when the truth was made public, very little changed in the narrative.

The truth of our moment is that the truth—veracity, facts, science—is no match for white ressentiment. Peaceful protesters remain, for that constituency of white America, subject to criminalization, which means, inevitably, that they remain subject to state—in its full, ideological sense—retribution. This aggrieved white constituency, angered as they are by any form of minority advancement (blacks, immigrants, Muslims, and others are all targets of their wrath, the objects of their vitriol), this constituency was empowered by the Trump White House, even in the wake of Trump's electoral defeat and the right-wing media's call to take action. So that they might "save their country," one presumes. To save this country from us, people like you and me, black

---

1. https://www.cnn.com/2020/08/28/politics/michelle-obama-jacob-blake-kenosha/index.html.

people, just for starters. It is, however, surprising how often that is their point of departure, though, isn't it?

This white constituency, whom Trump did not create but certainly *emboldened* (as the events of January 6, 2021, clearly showed), is by no means a new political phenomenon. What distinguishes them is that they had a bullhorn in the White House and a concerted right-wing news outlet, Fox, in its many iterations (I include right-wing AM radio in this designation), which allows for greater reverberation across the airwaves and in social media. They also have a deep demographic fear, one they can barely pronounce. They fear what is imminent—and immanent. The United States is in the process of becoming a white majority minority state, sometimes referred to as the "browning of America." Whites are about to become a minority in a country that they have always considered, with no good historical reason, "theirs." In a world where rapid change is the order of the day and the American empire is in visible decline, the truth of living in a waning hegemon is proving too powerful a reality for even the most hardnosed nationalists. Why else would they cling so desperately to the fiction that is "Make America Great Again"?

It is this entangled morass of fear, xenophobia, nostalgia for empire, and nativism that is ballasted by centuries of white supremacy. It is this existential fear, "existential" in their minds, at least, that spurs the right wing to unleash their virulence—physical as well as rhetorical—on those protesters they consider, in their terms, "looters," "rioters," all of whom are urged on by "socialists"—or, without distinction, "communists." At best, or worst, these "socialists" are members of the Democratic Party. If only we lived in a world of Democratic socialists. If only.

The white right pronounces the protesters "impatient" because they will not wait for the legal system to do its work. Except, of course, no one deemed Breonna Taylor, Ahmaud Arbery, or George Floyd worthy of the right to due process.

Justice is reserved for cops, preferably white cops. Under the guise of a police Bill of Rights. "Blue Lives Matter."

The "due process brigade" are old hat to the protesters. The pro-

testers, in their many and varied formations, are well versed in that old Led Zeppelin refrain. They already know the outcome. Best to just hum along with Robert Plant: "The song remains the same."

The protesters know, and they will be especially familiar with this if they are fans of the NBA's Kawhi Leonard and his mute New Balance advertisement, how things end. The police officer, or officers, as is often the case, is acquitted. Law, as it contorts itself to serve the ends most advantageous to white police officers, and order, as in retaining the status quo, can be relied upon to carry the day. The American justice system works, its advocates, who come in many stripes, insist. Indeed, it works, except for those who are not white. Everyone gets their day in court, free to make their case before a jury of their peers. Everyone is guaranteed a fair trial. Everyone, that is, except the dead or paralyzed or brutalized black body.

Emmett Till. Black America remembers, to this day.

At the end of Derrick Chauvin's trial, Emmett Till's family joined in sympathy with George Floyd's.

The Mississippi River divides the Twin Cities. St. Paul on the river's east bank, Minneapolis on its west. With George Floyd's murder, twenty-first-century Minneapolis finds itself yoked by shared black death to the Civil Rights struggle of the mid-1950s.

John Lewis. Civil Rights activist, congressman, Lewis paid the price, with a cracked skull, for daring to cross the Edmund Pettus bridge.

Addie Mae Collins (14), Cynthia Wesley (14), Carole Robertson (14), and Carol Denise McNair (11), killed in September 1963 at the 16th Street Baptist Church, in Birmingham, Alabama.

Black America remembers not because things have changed, but because they have remained so unutterably the same—at least as it pertains to the vulnerability of black bodies to white law enforcement.

The "indefatigability" of black memory. The burden of "indefatigability."

Muhammad Ali bore that burden with bravado, insouciance, and no small amount of anticolonial defiance. In 1967 Ali refused the draft, his logic unimpeachable, never to be forgotten: "I ain't got no quarrel with them Viet Cong, they never called me nigger. They never lynched me."

Tommie Smith (gold) and John Carlos (bronze) made their opposition visible, inscribing their militancy in silence. They let their gloved hands do the antiracist talking.[2] Together, that is, with the white Australian Peter Norman (silver), who stood in solidarity with them. Norman displayed his Olympic Project for Human Rights badge prominently (as did Smith and Carlos), as though he was as proud to oppose U.S. racism as he was to have clinched his silver medal in the 1968 200m dash. When Norman died in 2006 in Melbourne, Australia, Smith and Carlos served as pall bearers. This is how athletes who long ago stood together on a podium in Mexico City, who stood for justice and against state violence, honor each other in death. They walk in silent solidarity, as they once stood back-to-back all those years ago, silent, face turned against the world.

2. At the 2021 Olympics in Tokyo, Costa Rican gymnast Luciana Alvarado repeated Smith and Carlos's gesture. https://nypost.com/2021/07/28/costa-rican-gymnast-raises-fist-for-black-lives-matter-during-floor-routine.

14. Change Is Everywhere, Even the NHL

THE NHL, as even the most casual observer can tell, is overwhelmingly white and dominated by Canadian and European players (the NHL is only slightly more than 26 percent American).[1] However, not even the NHL could escape the effect of the Bucks' boycott. On August 26, the NHL went ahead with its three scheduled games. The Boston Bruins game against the Tampa Bay Lightning paused for a "moment of reflection," but that was all. The NHL found itself roundly criticized by athletes in other sports, as Major League Soccer, in addition to MLB and the NBA, called off its games.

Even within the NHL fraternity, there was unhappiness. A former NHL goaltender who played for the New York Islanders, the Los Angeles Kings, and the San Jose Sharks, Kelly Hrudey, offered a thoughtful a critique of the NHL's inaction on August 26. Or, rather, its action—that is, its decision to keep playing while the other leagues did not. Currently broadcasting for the Calgary Flames and working as an analyst for that venerable institution, "Hockey Night in Canada," Hrudey was unambiguous:

> "I don't think we should be here. I think the NHL should postpone the games," Hrudey said on a TV hit on NHL Canadian rights-holder

1. https://www.quanthockey.com/nhl/nationality-totals/nhl-players-2019-20-stats.html. Canadian players dominate, followed by the United States and Sweden.

Sportsnet before puck drop at Scotiabank Arena. "I really feel we should be more supportive of Black Lives Matter.

"I know for myself, instead of watching hockey, I'd prefer to be having this conversation with my family."[2]

The next day, Hrudey got his wish. The NHL, following the NBA and the WNBA, postponed their games for August 27th and 28th. This decision came on the heels of the NHL finding itself under attack from within. Because the Hockey Diversity Alliance (HDA) openly questioned the NHL's decision to proceed with games on August 26, the HDA, founded to increase racial diversity in the NHL, expressed their displeasure with the NHL's inaction. Two black Canadian players, Evander Kane (a winger on the Sharks) and Matt Dumba (a defense man for the Minnesota Wild), were at the forefront of the efforts to make change tack.

On August 27, photographs taken from within the NHL bubble emerged. All the teams publicly expressed their support for social justice. A veritable United Nations of Western players joined forces, with Canada, the United States, Sweden, Finland, the Czech Republic, Germany, and even tiny Slovenia (with a single player) metonymically represented. One suspects that until the game gains a foothold in minority communities in North America and Europe (where, simply because of the size of the population and the relatively small landmass compared to the United States, the rise of minority representation might be more likely and happen more quickly), the NHL will have a tough row to hoe. For the foreseeable future, it is likely that the fight for social justice will remain the primary responsibility of black Canadians, the odd American or black European player, and the politically progressive white player—regardless of national origin.

At the very least, however, what social pressure and the HDA were able to achieve in the wake of the Bucks' actions demonstrates

2. https://www.huffingtonpost.ca/entry/nhl-nba-boycott_ca_5f47b-32fc5b6cf66b2b42914.

that, its demographics notwithstanding, the NHL is not immune to the racial politics that obtain in North America.

Indeed, no sport is. Even NASCAR is subject to the forces calling for social justice, as we have seen.

Sometimes, it takes a team. Or, at least, it takes an individual to lead her or his team. Sometimes, everything is epic. It depends upon the singular athlete.

15. Biting the Hand That Feeds Them

So why not take a stand, Premier League players? Why not also speak directly to those in power? Imagine the impact of star players, who we know have a social conscience, taking the lead in raising concerns about oppressive regimes buying Premier League clubs, and directing these concerns at their own potential paymasters.

— BARNEY RONAY, *The Guardian*

IF THE NHL, a racially hegemonic sport (with its strong European contingent) can rise, albeit a little belatedly, to the challenge of confronting social justice, can the English Premier League (football) bring itself to take up the problem that is American owners who support Donald Trump. In a football continent where organizations such as "Kick It Out" have long (relative to other environs) worked to ensure an antiracist culture, where strict punishments are imposed on clubs and, indeed, entire national football associations for racist acts by players, administrators, coaching staff, and fans (and, most pertinent to this discussion, where the vast majority of players showed their support for the social justice movement in the United States by taking a knee before kick-off and clubs emblazoned "Black Lives Matter" on the back of their jerseys in the first game back after the pandemic), can the players—and not only the black players but, again, they may have to take the lead—turn their focus on those owners whose support for Trump goes entirely contrary to the politics of the Premier League? Since it is precisely these owner's financial backing that made Trump's ascent possible and unleashed a new level of racial toxicity on minorities.

Caught squarely in the crosshairs here are those players who draw their paychecks from the likes of Arsenal, Crystal Palace, and Manchester United, players who, United's Marcus Rashford chief among them, showed themselves possessed of an acute "social conscience." (During the pandemic, Rashford showed himself to be the footballer who rebuked the United Kingdom's Conservative government for its failure to deliver food to hungry children. Rashford was, as he should have been, widely lauded for this.)[1] Arsenal's Stan Kroenke funded Trump's inauguration to the tune of $1 million. One wonders if Arsenal's Mesut Özil,[2] outspoken critic of the Chinese Communist Party's policy on the Uighurs, would be willing to make his opposition to Kroenke's consorting with a leader who considers Black Lives Matter a "terrorist organization" known, publicly.

I expect not, in part because Özil and Ilkay Gundogan of Manchester City have both made public their support for the Turkish leader Recep Tayyip Erdoğan, a position that saw them come under attack from those opposed to Erdoğan's dictatorial rule.[3] After all, Özil (as well as Gundogan) was steadfastly silent when Erdoğan's government issued an arrest for Turkish basketball player Enes Kanter (Boston Celtics) because of Kanter's criticism of Erdoğan. We are left to conclude, then, that Özil is politically outspoken only addressing issues that pertain directly to his identity. His politics reveal themselves as predictable and narrowly identitarian; what we are dealing with then is not politics, in any substantive sense, but identitarianism. This makes his

1. https://www.msn.com/en-gb/news/uknews/marcus-rashford-clashes-with-tory-mp-over-child-food-poverty/ar-BB18Lcsz?ocid=uxbndl-bing.

2. Özil has subsequently left Arsenal. He now plays for Fenerbahçe in Turkey.

3. Erdogan was the best man at Ozil's wedding. https://www.bbc.com/news/world-europe-48564192.

position on the Uighurs no less important but, for all that, reveals him as a man with a severely restricted or identitarian "social conscience." Who among Arsenal's array of players will step up and meet the demands of the moment? Will it be their Gabonese captain, Pierre-Emerick Aubameyang? Their German goalkeeper Bernd Leno? Or, will it be one of their black young guns? Joe Willock, Ainsley Maitland-Niles, or Bukayo Saka? How much do black lives matter to black players at Arsenal?

Crystal Palace's co-owner Josh Harris spent some of his time advising the Trump administration. Will the perennially dissatisfied Wilfried Zaha—a talented player who perpetually accuses opponents of singling him out for special treatment, a player who is always agitating for a move away from Palace, a star winger who changed his national affiliation from England to Côte d'Ivoire—be the spokesperson who takes Harris to lead a Palace coup? Or will it the black Belgian striker Christian Benteke or the black English winger, Andros Townsend?[4] What about Palace's Serbian captain, Luka Milivojević?

Manchester United's club director Ed Glazer is well known as a fundraiser for Trump. Since Rashford cut his political teeth on the pandemic, he might be best positioned to take up the cudgels in this new struggle. United's white English captain, Harry Maguire, who is not averse to falling foul of the law, at least the Greek law, could put his contrarian streak to good use and lead the way for the United Against Trump movement. France's Anthony Martial, Spain's David de Gea and Juan Mata, and United's host of black English players, Aaron Wan-Bissaka and Mason Greenwould, as well as their white English teammate, Luke Shaw, would surely follow.

Are there any players opposed to taking the field against clubs that materially support Trump? Liverpool's captain, Jordan Henderson, who rallied all the Premier League skippers and then

---

4. Townsend left Crystal Palace at the end of 2020–21 season to join Everton.

the players in support Britain's National Health System, presents himself as a logical leader. After all, if the pandemic has taught the world anything, it is that universal healthcare should be a right. A fundamental right. Minorities, as the pandemic revealed so starkly, are measurably more vulnerable to the health (and socioeconomic) ravages of the pandemic.

Which Premier League footballer, from this club or any other, is willing to bite the hand that feeds them?

And, while we're at it, is it possible to imagine all international footballers boycotting the next World Cup in Qatar because of its ethnocentric monarchy? Or, Qatari labor practices as it pertains to the millions of migrant workers who are subject to appalling conditions? Extreme heat, the confiscation of passports, the poor living conditions? These, as we well know, are the self-same workers who are building the stadia and the other facilities to ensure that the World Cup takes place in the gas-and-oil-rich Qatar, a state with no real football history of which to speak. Why should the players not demand a full and accurate accounting of FIFA, the sport's governing body, finances? What's to stop the players from standing up for human rights the world over by putting the World Cup on hold?

When George Floyd was murdered, the late Rush Limbaugh, the high priest of white supremacy, could not defend Derek Chauvin. Rush Limbaugh, I repeat, as ardent and unreconstructed a racist as this country has thrown up over the centuries. And yet the state's attack on black life has not abated in the time since.

Similarly, the white, right-wing televangelist Pat Robertson denounced the death of Adam Toledo.

Nip, at almost the exact moment that the jury in the Chauvin case found him guilty on all three counts, police in Columbus, Ohio, shot sixteen-year-old Ma'Khia Bryant, an African American teenager in foster care, four times.[5] She died shortly afterwards.

---

5. https://www.msn.com/en-us/news/us/makhia-bryant-columbus-

According to reports, Bryant, who was armed with a knife (which some say she dropped before she was shot), was involved in an altercation with another girl.

In the same situation, how many white teenagers—more precisely, suburban white teenagers—would have come to the same bloody end as Bryant?

In relation to the black body, the law of policing is inviolate: shoot first, shoot often. No force is "disproportionate" in relation to the black body.

Bryant was killed some twenty minutes before Chauvin's conviction.

No one makes a better case for the abolition of policing more effectively, and viscerally, than the police themselves.

It needs to be said again: the police cannot be reformed.

In light of this ongoing police brutality, with protesters shot in Austin, Texas; Omaha, Nebraska; and Kenosha, Wisconsin; I wonder, Ezra, how could any thinking person continue to support Trump? Even countenance voting for him, as more than seventy-four million did in the 2020 election?

However, just when I am on the verge of being appalled and disgusted, I remind myself that in this country it is important to never underestimate the depth and intensity of white hatred for the black body. One should never be shocked at a certain constituency of white America's capacity to sustain itself through such hatred.

From the white supremacist rallies that took place all over the country in the summer of 2020, rallies in places such as Oneida, New York (a flotilla of Trump supporters wearing MAGA hats and waving American flags with goose-stepping gusto), to a white supremacist teenager understanding himself free to take black lives in the cause of protecting property. There is a snarling hatred in those white faces.

They hate us. Such a recognition is in no way new to you or me.

---

police-release-body-camera-footage-in-shooting-of-16-year-old/ar-BB1fRK-Ju?ocid=uxbndlbing.

What Trump did (continues to do, even as he is out of office) is give white hatred presidential cover. In so doing, he has fueled this hatred. He has succeeded in elevating this hatred to a new pitch, a fevered pitch. So now we live, Nip, in a cauldron of white anger and resentment. Black America (as well as other minorities, Asians especially so in the wake of the pandemic) finds itself vulnerable, simultaneously afraid of white violence and motivated to act against this violence. Has Trump reached some ungodly plateau, where the white supremacist gods convene in order to decide our fate?

They murder us and then they, shamelessly, blame us for our anger.

It is this, my son, that I want to explain to all those Premier League footballers in the employ of Arsenal, Crystal Palace, and Manchester United. This is what their bosses fund. As much as Paris St. Germain, owned by the Qataris, are the beneficiaries of the exploitation and devastation of migrant lives; as much as Manchester City are built on money derived from a range of dubious capital ventures undertaken by the United Arab Emirates royal family.

There are no innocents here, my son. All are culpable.

Hatred of the black body is what Kroenke, Harris, and Glazer, through their various underwritings of Trump, fermented. It is this hatred that makes black life so disposable to the white supremacist mobs.

It is tempting to suggest that this pathological hatred of the black body confounds reason. However, such an argument overlooks the lived reality that racism in no way depends upon logic for its activation and sustenance. Racism is, in this way, an autoforce (or, at the risk of contradicting myself, it is an autologic). Racism is entirely capable of powering itself, and renewing itself, seemingly without end.

Why not hold the World Cup hostage to human rights? Could there be a better cause?

Why would footballers not want to test the system to the limits of their—and its—power?

Why would they not want to be an instrument for good (justice in its many forms) in the world and, in doing so, make common cause with athletes, all athletes, possibly, the world over?

Refusing to participate in games, especially those that are part of a global spectacle (World Cup, Champions League, the Euros, Africa Cup of Nations, and so on), might address the critique leveled by the Queens Park Rangers (QPR) director, Les Ferdinand. Black British and a former England international, Ferdinand explained the QPR players' decision not to take a knee before their games in the Championship (the second tier of English football). For QPR and Ferdinand, taking a knee amounts to little more than an empty, superficial gesture. It performs, in the most pejorative sense, antiracism while doing little to nothing to effect structural change. Either in the game itself or society at large.[6]

Taking a knee as symbolic protest. Yet another reformist gesture.

For his part, Ferdinand is demanding sustainable, material change.

QPR, then, as scoring one against reformism.

QPR, bucking the trend, refusing the gestural as appropriate to the historic demands of the moment.

I doubt George Hill is a fan of English football, but Les Ferdinand should sign him up.

At the very least, Ferdinand should send Hill a QPR shirt.

Hill would look good in QPR's blue and white hoops.

Why would the footballers not want to, if not take up single-handedly, then stand in solidarity with other black athletes, align themselves with that famed Mexico City trio? Why would other athletes, especially in the wake of what George Hill's Bucks did, not commit themselves to the same set of principles?

Footballers of the world unite. You have everything to lose.

Isn't that the only condition under which politics should be conducted? In an earlier era, such a decision, such collective action, would have gone by an honorable name: "revolution."

6. https://edition.cnn.com/2020/09/22/football/qpr-taking-a-knee-les-ferdinand-spt-intl/index.html#:~:text=QPR%20said%20the%20decision%20for%20players%20not%20to,goal%20in%20their%203-2%20defeat%20by%20Coventry%20City.

If only a black athlete could revive that prospect. Like John Carlos and Tommie Smith.

Like Peter Norman, the white Australian athlete ostracized by his national athletic federation—and many of his fellow-Australians—for supporting Carlos and Smith.

It is better to stand in solidarity with the protesting black bodies than acquiesce to racism. It is better go to your grave borne by honorable athletic comrades than to live a morally compromised life.

Will the Premier League throw up a Peter Norman?

I'm looking at you, Jordan Henderson. I'm asking you, my favorite Wearsider, to tap into the left-wing spirit of that old Scottish socialist whose statue stands proudly outside Anfield. He used to go by the name of "Bill Shankly." "Football is not a matter of life or death," Shanks said, "it is much more important than that."

He stood with Scouser workers, did Shanks.

Who will you stand with, Hendo? The moment for decision is now, Jordan.

We pride ourselves, we Liverpool FC fans, on being the "club of the people." Tough, working class, Liverpudlians, we stood against Thatcher and her dastardly anti-union politics. We speak a distinct, and distinctly radical, political language. Albeit in an accent non-Scousers find impenetrable.

Remember Robbie Fowler's support for the stevedores? He was fined for it. He cared not a jot. A proud, native son of Liverpool, is Robbie, doing his bit to let the dockworkers on Merseyside know that they were not alone in their struggle.

Let's do the right thing, Hendo. We're looking to you. You are heir to a venerable radical tradition.

The moment in history may have arrived when we can remain the "club of the people" only if the captain of Liverpool F.C. exceeds our orbit and agitates on behalf of exploited migrant labor in Doha, or any else in the world, for that matter. Workers of the world, unite, you have everything to gain. Bill Shankly was born in Scotland, but at his political core he was a Scouser: anti-authoritarian, a champion of and for the working class.

For now, Jordan, bringing attention to exploitation of foreign labor and the denigration of human life in Qatar will do.

As a start.[7]

7. Jordan Henderson has, I find myself now—happily—having to add, stepped up. Not once, but twice. First Hendo made it clear that racism is not the (primary, my qualification, not his) responsibility of its victims but that of the perpetrators. White racists have to hold themselves accountable, as must those whites who understand themselves to be antiracist. Also, following the June 28, 2021, Euro 20 (the tournament was postponed for a year because of the pandemic) game between England and Germany, Hendo spoke out in defense of an LGBTQ England fan who had been harassed on the grounds of sexuality. Every England fan, Hendo declared, should be free to cheer for their team without fear of harassment. Hendo has come through.

16. A Pause for a Cause

WHICH ATHLETE, watching, on any media platform, in any part of the world, could not have been struck by the ontological exhaustion that is the black athlete's burden to bear in America?

Interviewed on CNN by Anderson Cooper, former NBA stalwart Chris Webber expressed his support for current players and hailed the actions they had taken on the 26th of August. Webber, who from his perch as TNT commentator had spoken movingly on the 26th against the backdrop of the abandoned hardwood, lauded the interruption—the disruption, if you will—that the players had enacted. By boycotting the games, Webber wanted it recognized, they gave everyone the opportunity to reflect on the players' rationale. In the moment that was the pause, it was now incumbent on America to address why the players had decided to champion the antipolice brutality cause. Webber wanted America to do undertake the work of explicating, to itself, why the players had chosen to do what they did.

In setting the nation this difficult task, Webber wanted to break the cycle of media expectation where every "expert," no matter how unqualified, is given license to hold forth. Dire prognostications, wholesale declamations (embodied in no figure more viscerally, or loudly, than ESPN's cartoonish Stephen A. Smith), and saccharine invocations too often dominate in the moment of the crisis.

In his sober vulnerability (he seemed on the verge of tears), Webber's hope was for something very different. Webber's was a call for the kind of national self-reflection in order that that something else, something like an honest reckoning with the ongoing effects of racism, in its many iterations, might become possible. Webber's was a plea, and yet it had all the trappings of nonexpectation. What he was calling for would not come to pass. His words could not disguise his hopelessness. His words were betrayed by the brittle timbre of his voice. Like many others, he had seen this movie before.

In a word, Webber spoke like a black man overwhelmed by the daily reality of being black in America. Almost a year later, in his op-ed for the *New York Times,* the African American columnist Charles M. Blow gives voice to Webber's barely suppressed hopelessness. "Society," Blow writes, "has become desensitized to the killing of Black men."[1] Bereft of alternatives, Blow declares: "Rage is the only language I have left."[2]

What Webber, less than twenty-four hours after the boycott, called for, had already been embodied by his TNT colleague Kenny "the Jet" Smith. Overwhelmed at the news of the boycott, cognizant of what it meant, Smith, who won two championships with the Houston Rockets, could barely speak:

> "Right now my head is ready to explode like in the thought of what's going on," Smith told his co-hosts Ernie Johnson, Shaquille O'Neal, and Charles Barkley. "I don't know if I'm appropriate enough to say it what the players are feeling and how they're feeling. I haven't talked to any player."
>
> "Even driving here and getting into the studio . . . hearing calls and people talking. . . . And for me, I think the biggest thing now . . . as a black man as a former player, I think it's best for me to support the players and just not to be here tonight . . . And I figure out what happens after that."[3]

1. Charles M. Blow, "Rage Is the Only Language I Have Left," *New York Times,* April 17, 2021.

2. Blow, "Rage."

3. https://www.theguardian.com/sport/2020/aug/26/kenny-smith-nba-on-tnt-walk-off-basketball-tv.

With that, "the Jet" disconnected his mike, and walked off the set of TNT's Pregame Show. As a fan of the "Pregame Show," I appreciate the host Ernie Johnson's equanimity and his trademark bowties. I am agnostic about Shaquille O'Neal. In truth, I tolerate him. However, I love "Sir Charles," the "Round Mound of Rebound." Charles Barkley is irreverent, at once opinionated and self-deprecatory, given to a grandiosity that is destined to blow up in his face.

Things are more vexed for me with "the Jet." I appreciate his keen insights, and his race to the "board" at halftime always raises a smile. My difficulties with Kenny Smith stem from his playing days. Kenny, you see, broke my heart in 1994 when he was the point guard on that Rockets team that beat my New York Knickerbockers. My Knicks took it all the way to game 7, but, courtesy of Knicks shooting guard John Starks's voracious ineptitude, we fell short. Taking 3 after 3, one clanging off the rim more thunderously than the other, Starks just kept launching 3s. Sometimes, in the dead of night, I can still see Starks lining up to shoot yet one more three. Starks was nothing at all like Kenny. "The Jet" was all discipline and calm. All poise at the point, dictating play while the Knicks flailed. As you've already discerned, Kenny Smith is the stuff of my Knicks nightmares.

And I cannot tell you how many of those nightmares I have, Ezra. One day I will tell you the story of Charles Smith's offensive futility. Against the Chicago Bulls, yes, the Jordan Bulls. And Horace Grant's defense. And the heartbreak. And the Sisyphean quality of Patrick "the Juggernaut" Ewing's vain struggle to carry the Knicks to a championship. To say nothing of Ewing's struggles at the free throw line. As I told you, son, this is the reason it took me so long to watch ESPN's documentary on the Bulls, The Last Dance. *I could not watch it with you, much as you implored me to. To this day, there is still so much pain there.*

17. Ontological Exhaustion

STRANGELY or, maybe, appropriately, it is "Sir Charles" who bridges Webber to Smith. Speaking, cherubically on CNN on the 26th of August, Barkley nailed it: ontological exhaustion:

> The bottom line is it is exhausting being Black, especially when you are a celebrity.
>   You know, I love Tom Brady [quarterback on the NFL's Tampa Bay Buccaneers] but nobody asks him about what is going on in white America. Nobody asks Luca Doncic about what's going on in America.[1]

Well Charles, probably a little unfair to ask a Slovene (Doncic) "about what is going on in America." America did have a Slovenian First Lady who is hardly a representative of the Ljubljana intelligentsia, a considerable force in the world of contemporary philosophy. So, on that score alone, Luca deserves a pass. Nonetheless, if we substitute "Doncic" for any other white player in the NBA . . . they would not be asked for their thoughts on white living prospects in Boise, Idaho. So, point taken, "Sir Charles."

Your "Doncic" reference must not be allowed to detract attention from the core issue you are raising. Ontological exhaustion.

1. https://www.msn.com/en-us/sports/nba/charles-barkley-the-bottom-line-is-it-is-exhausting-being-black/ar-BB18qQsP?ocid=spartan-dhp-feeds.

To be ontologically exhausted is to be tired to the very essence of your being. Tired to your bones, as they say; completely spent, resources—personal and communal—utterly depleted. It is also by no means limited to "celebrities," LeBron, Serena, or public figures such as "the Jet" and "Sir Charles." Ontological exhaustion is no respecter of rank. To be black in America is, for every black person, always to live either as ontologically exhausted or to be on the verge of it. From "Boy Willie" ("The Piano Lesson" to Vera and Louise "Seven Guitars"), August Wilson's "Century Cycle"—ten plays documenting black life, one in each decade of the twentieth century—is full of world-weary, almost-completely-beaten-down-by-life black characters. Only death puts an end to this exhaustion. Too often prematurely.

Nevertheless, again, "Sir Charles," point taken. Every black person who is in any way publicly visible—a "celebrity"—in America has to endure what I have named elsewhere the "burden of over-representation."[2] The single black person, presumed to be an exceptional black person, must speak for the entire black community, must give voice to the aspirations, fears, and the lived experience of that community. Jackie Robinson bore that burden. As did Althea Gibson, as did Jack Johnson—more than one hundred years ago. And, like you, "Sir Charles," Jack Johnson did so with more than a dollop of mischief. In fact, "Papa Jack" was more than willing to spit in the eye of white America. Sometimes through a gold-toothed smile.

The burden of over-representation also means, "Sir Charles," that when you speak of ontological exhaustion, you speak in our collective name. You speak as us. You speak for us. We are all tired.

This does not mean, however, that we ever get to say "Enough." That option is not available to us. We begin again, as if for the first time.

---

2. See Grant Farred, *The Burden of Over-representation: Race, Sport, Philosophy* (Philadelphia: Temple University Press, 2018).

We begin again in the philosophical spirit of Peter Sloterdijk, cognizant of Ella Baker's injunction, once more inflected by Jayson Tatum's winsome nostalgia. What Tatum discovered was the joy of being contained within. The NBA bubble as the experience of dwelling in containment, "confined" to and by utopia.

And because it is impossible for those opposed to racism to ever declare themselves done with it as long as it is alive, it is all the more important to conduct a struggle on the principle of dual power.

A principle that remains ever true to utopia as not only possibility, but as absolute—"compelling"—necessity.

Indeed, if possible, it would be best to begin again—for this first time, as it were—by conducting a dual struggle. To fight for electoral representation while working, simultaneously, to supersede representative democracy with a society in which radical equality and justice—that is, an equality manifested in every walk of life— holds sway.

18. Inverse Displacement

ACCORDING TO TNT'S ERNIE JOHNSON, the then-L.A. Clippers' head coach Glenn "Doc" Rivers is a "joyful man." (Rivers was fired by the Clippers after they lost in the playoffs to the Denver Nuggets. He now coaches the Philadelphia 76ers.) And, in my recollection of him as a player, "Doc" is a witty man possessed of a keen sense of humor. Between 1994 and 1996, "Doc" was the point guard on the New York Knicks, where he formed an effective partnership with the Knicks center, Patrick Ewing. When "Doc" and Ewing were teammates, he proclaimed the "Juggernaut" (as Walt Clyde Frazier dubbed Ewing) the "best center in the NBA." In 1996 Rivers was traded to San Antonio, where he would play with a new center, David Robinson. Asked about the trade, Rivers quipped: "Patrick Ewing isn't the best center in the NBA anymore." "Doc" knew just how to win favor with his big man, wherever he went.

Interviewed on August 25, 2020, after his Clippers had demolished Doncic's Dallas Mavericks to the tune of 154–111, Rivers spoke forcefully. With a breaking heart, Rivers held forth, in some moments overcome by anger, in others offering a candid snapshot of racism and segregation in the United States, and in still others, he just sounds like a black man utterly depleted by living in America. This is—once more—an encounter with both ontological exhaustion and the burden of over-representation:

> What stands out to me is just watching the Republican Convention. They're spewing this fear, right? You hear Donald Trump and all of them talking about fear. We're the ones getting killed. We're the ones getting shot. We're the ones that were denied to live in certain communities. We've been hung. We've been shot. All you do is keep hearing about fear. It's amazing to me why we keep loving this country, and this country does not love us back. It's really so sad. I should just be a coach.[1]

Rightly, or wrongly, that choice is not available to "Doc" Rivers. He will never "just be a coach." That is the burden that has fallen to him, Chris Webber, Charles Barkley and Kenny Smith—inter alia. In moments such as these, the black coach, the black color commentator, the black TV analyst, will all be called upon to summon up, from both their immediate past and from the deepest recesses of their being, the courage, understanding of history, and the necessary command of language to address social injustice.

Salient about Rivers's inveighing against racism, is his willingness to critique, directly, and in person, "Donald Trump" and white Republican "hypocrisy," although "hypocrisy" seems a trifle insufficient to the violence and racism unleased by the GOP. "They're spewing fear" by generating hatred. All the while, Rivers points out, it turns out that the "fear" is baseless. In quick, short, declarative statements, Rivers lists an itinerary of the violence done, still being done, to black lives, going all the way back to Jim Crow America: "We're the ones getting killed. We're the ones getting shot. We're the ones that were denied to live in certain communities. We've been hung. We've been shot. All you do is keep hearing about fear."

The most pernicious aspect of Trump's white fearmongering is that the effect of this inverse displacement is that racist white America is now endorsed, with the presidential seal of approval, to (continue to) act against black bodies. Inverse displacement, or, perverse displacement, is nothing other than the license to kill black

1. https://www.rev.com/blog/transcripts/doc-rivers-speech-transcript-on-jacob-blake-rnc-police-being-black-in-america.

bodies. Brutal police officers, teenage white vigilantes (from out of state, brandishing a semi-automatic), camouflaged white vigilantes (Michigan, see below), white militia, and gun-toting white men of all ages, are free to act (again, see below.) In the name of (their) "fear."

Once more, Rivers offers a pointed response:

> Yo, it's funny. We protest and they send riot guards, right? They sent people in riot outfits. They go to Michigan with guns and they're spitting on cops, and nothing happens. The training has to change in the police force. The unions have to be taken down in the police force.[2]

Perverse displacement mutates, seamlessly, into (racially motivated) disproportionate force. Black peaceful "protest" must be put down by "people in riot outfits." A fake $20 bill got George Floyd killed, but militias, and their kindred folk, "spit on cops and nothing happens." Glenn Anton "Doc" Rivers, the son of a Chicago policeman, a black man not in favor of defunding the police force, instructs the nation into exactly how systemic racism works in the United States. This is what two systems of justice looks like.

"Yo, it's not funny."

Even though Rivers starts out agitating for institutional reform ("The training has to change in the police force"), he quickly transitions to a more radical—and necessary—critique. It is the police unions, including the Police Benevolent Association of the City of New York,[3] the largest police union in the nation, the Delaware Fraternal Order of Police[4] and the Colorado State Lodge of the Fraternal Order of Police,[5] that are determined to hold the "thin blue line." It is the police unions where union chiefs such as Trump

2. https://www.rev.com/blog/transcripts/doc-rivers-speech-transcript-on-jacob-blake-rnc-police-being-black-in-america.

3. https://www.businessinsider.com/biggest-p.

4. https://www.delawareonline.com/story/news/2020/09/05/delaware-fraternal-order-of-police-endorses-trump-president-responds/5728007002/den-2020-9.

5. https://www.denverpost.com/2020/09/04/colorado-police-union-trump-endorsement/.

supporter Bob Kroll of the Minneapolis police union are genetically ill-disposed to systemic reform. (Kroll called George Floyd a "violent criminal.")[6] It is the police, either in the course of doing their routine police work or through the protection they enjoy from their (racist and) retrograde unions, the buffer against punishment that is the police Bill of Rights, that give the black community, and all minority communities, every reason to distrust them. The black body that approaches the police (also known as a "voluntary" engagement or interaction), the black body that is approached by the police (an "involuntary" interaction), always does with and in fear. Fear of brutality, fear of death. The police union that endorses Trump seeks to do nothing but buy itself lifetime immunity against prosecution.

Trump has given white police officers what they most desire—a blank blue check. Under Trump, white police officers were presidentially licensed to kill black bodies. Explicitly. There should be no mistaking it. Trump and the police unions are cut from the same sadistic ideological cloth. They are driven by the same brutal impulses—black life is of no consequence.

Within this context, against the backdrop of the 2020 Republican convention, the Bucks' slogan, "Fear the Deer," takes on the appearance of a whimsy.

How far can antiracist America go before it encounters the vigilantes of white "fear?" As far as a gun-wielding white, teenage vigilante will let them go before shooting them.

White racism, as I argued, makes no demands on reason. If it did, how would it be able to respond, with any honesty, to Rivers's interrogative? White Americans, in their many guises, are doing the killing—as they did the lynching, as they did the redlining, as they continue to do it. White America, Coach Rivers, is "spewing fear."

Black America knows well enough: fear the white Republican. Fear the white Republican who votes for Trump. Fear Trump: that is where black fear, in this moment, begins. But it does not end there. Fear, because they have jurisdiction in your neighborhood, police officers,

6. https://heavy.com/news/2020/06/bob-kroll/.

any police officers, you might be unlucky enough to encounter—they are backed by a Trumpian union.

It is here, in his denunciation of police unions, that Rivers's and Jameson's arguments converge. *Police brutality, police unions that protect their own at the expense of black life, police unions endorsing Trump, is inured against "decisive tinkerings." It is certainly beyond "systemic change."*

It is not, then, merely a matter of reforming or defunding the police. *The primary axis of dual power (if we designate representative democracy as the secondary one, the axis must be superannuated) turns on the work of organizing a society in which there is neither a need nor a function for the police.*

It is only through dual power that it becomes possible to relieve society entirely of the need to engage questions about policing. To posit a utopian outcome: the goal is a society free of policing. The work of utopian thinking is to present possibilities for how to achieve this desired end. That is the challenge that, according to Sloterdijk, philosophy must confront. Urgently. In the most successful Jamesonian eventuation we project a society free of policing. That is the only guarantee of a society free of police brutality.

For now we can say that "Doc" Rivers has, inadvertently, taken the first step on this—on his own—utopian path. By aiming his critique at the seat of police power, by calling for the elimination of police unions, Rivers offers the prospect of ending policing, disuniting police power. If the police union is eliminated, then it becomes possible to fracture the whole into a series of sedimented pieces that are accountable to specific constituencies—that is, to "federalize" it into individual precincts (at least, as the initial demand).

Fidelity to place, in Sloterdikj's terms, makes one subject to the ethos of the specific environment. To live "in situ" has a telling effect because "one establishes oneself in a particular place and extends oneself by means of local resonances."[7] All are made accountable to the "local resonances" of the "place" they inhabit.

7. Sloterdijk, *In the World*, 257.

In other words, treat police unions in the same way that legislation deals with corporate monopolies. Break them up. They are genetically wired to ensure the preservation of the right to white brutality against black bodies. Conquer police unions through division.

White America is spitting all manner of violence. And it is doing so under the guise of the police being "under attack." "Blue lives matter, *more*." Once again, we are witness to the workings of the perversity of inverse displacement. The police who commit willful acts of brutality, like those white supremacists and their varied state and media apparatuses, the police and the white militias who have the power to inspire fear, to stoke hatred and violently upend black life, cast themselves as, if not quite the victims of, the certainly as vulnerable to a black minority.

"The horror, the horror": inverse displacement is how the Conradian specter casts itself in America circa 2020.

The truth of fear is an American tragedy.

A tragedy for black America.

The continued destruction of black life is the only way in which white "fear" can be allayed. Those who perpetrate "fear" are asking for protection . . . from what? The fear they sow? Who has the right not to be "killed"? Or "hung"? Or "shot"?

19. Love, Unrequited

We keep loving this country. But this country doesn't
love us back.

—"DOC" RIVERS.

FOR ALL HIS INTERROGATIVE ACUITY, it is when he talks about
black America's unrequired love–"this country doesn't love us
back"—that Rivers comes closest to breaking down. Rivers's proximity to tears and affective dissolution, a potential public opening
up of the athlete that holds within it the risk of self-upending, a
potentiality detectable in Webber and Smith, is not the consequence
of "Doc's" illusions about American racism. It is not false consciousness, as such.

The depth of Rivers's feeling, rather, registers as shock. As dis-
belief. It is borne out the recognition of perpetual vulnerability.
Love, contextually rendered, as the right to equal protection under
the law:

My dad was a cop. I believe in good cops. We're not trying to defund
the police and take all their money away. We're trying to get them
to protect us, just like they protect everybody else. I didn't want
to talk about it before the game, because it's so hard, to just keep
watching it. That video, if you watch that video, you don't need to be
black to be outraged. You need to be American and outraged. How
dare the Republicans talk about fear? We're the ones that need to
be scared. We're the ones having to talk to every black child. What
white father has to give his son a talk about being careful if you get
pulled over? It's just ridiculous. It just keeps getting . . . It keeps
going. There's no charges. Brionna *[sic]* Taylor, no charges, nothing.

All we're asking is you live up to the Constitution. That's all we're asking, for everybody, for everyone.[1]

Rivers's discursive struggle, his grappling toward a language that can bear an intellectual weight dispersed over several key phenomena. These include his specific call for police reform, his love of country (patriotism seems too generalized a term), his existential fear ("We're the ones that need to be scared."), his deep sense of racial injustice ("We're the ones having to talk to every black child") and a pessimism that pervades his inveighing. Rivers's entire discursive apparatus, however, hinges upon a sense of betrayal that itself betrays an "original" fidelity to, faith in, the "Constitution." In this regard the political philosopher Charles Mills's argument for a paradigmatic understanding of the law—for a sociopolitical explication of the context in which the law does its work—bears engagement. For Mills, "normative debates about right and wrong, justice and injustice, typically involve not merely value disputes but competing narratives of what has happened in the past and what is happening right now, alternative descriptive frameworks and interpretations."[2] In a word, Mills distills the difficulty that Rivers is confronting: "competing narratives." There is no place in the white supremacist narrative for Rivers's legitimate "fears," for his incomprehension that those who perpetrate violence simultaneously claim the right to be "scared"—of the black body, inter alia; the white supremacist narrative is intent upon, U.S. Constitution or no, retaining for itself the rank of first among equals. The problem, however, with giving credence to "alternative descriptive frameworks and interpretations" is that it presupposes (at the very least, it creates the impression) that each of the "competing narratives"

1. https://www.rev.com/blog/transcripts/doc-rivers-speech-tran-script-on-jacob-blake-rnc-police-being-black-in-america.
2. Charles Mills, *Black Rights / White Wrongs: The Critique of Racial Liberalism* (New York: Oxford University Press, 2017), 114.

and "alternative descriptive frameworks and interpretations" are equally valid. That is, each can make an equal claim upon truth.

This is clearly not the case. There are only facts. "Alternative facts" is, at best, an oxymoron, at worst, a blatant lie. Rather than pitting the virtues (such as they are) of one "competing narrative" against another, the only way to proceed is to entirely deny the grounds of untruth. And to do so declaratively. Instead of piecemeal refutation, untruth should be met, in its very first articulation, with denunciation and refusal. To engage piecemeal is to invite further obfuscation, dissembling, and, at its worst, peroration. Because of his incomprehension (justifiable as it might be), Rivers—inadvertently, in a moment of pain and anguish—assumes, unwittingly, the burden of explicating the other (the police, police unions, white America), and, in the process, Rivers makes himself responsible for "narrativizing" the (black) self. More precisely, trying to make sense of the other's untruths. Best to dismiss it, outright. Better still to proclaim it, in the clearest possible terms, racist.

Held Hostage by the Constitution

It is in Rivers's expectation that, if American "lived up" to the terms of the "Constitution," he, as a black parent, would be spared the dreaded conversation about police brutality—"about being careful if you get pulled over"—and if the "Constitution" were adhered to there would be justice for "Breonna Taylor." Rivers understands the U.S. "Constitution" as the condition of possibility, so that the problem is not with the document itself but because it remains willfully unfulfilled by white supremacy. For his part, Jameson names the "American Constitution" a "counterrevolutionary document" that poses "unique problems."[3]

One of the main problems that the "American Constitution" presents is that it, as Jameson places a conceptual—we could also say

3. Jameson, "An American Utopia," 12.

intellectual—limit on how to reorganize society. The intention of any postrevolutionary document is to concentrate power within the new elite, to create bureaucratic structures that implement, exercise, and extend (if possible) this power, and, in so doing, to establish the founding document (enshrined as the virtuous articulation that marks the new beginning) as the (only) touchstone capable of redistributing, however minimally, power. Without threatening the enfranchised classes or enfranchising a new elite.

The "Constitution," as such, marks the limits of Rivers's imaginary, an imaginary faithful to the representative democracy, an imagination seeking to reform rather than undo power as such. Again, if we follow the logic of dual power, then it is entirely plausible to simultaneously endorse—loudly—Rivers's call for "constitutionality" while also working to antiquate the document by creating a new set of precepts by which to live differently. After all, if America is an "experiment" in social organization, if it is an "idea" of the nation rather than *Blut und Grund,* why should the number of "experiments" be curtailed, why should the possible array of ideas be restricted? If anything, does not the failure of the now in fact call for, urgently, a "revolutionary" rather than continued subscription to a "counterrevolutionary" document?

If the black athlete undertakes, with fortitude and stringent critique, to reform the system, then does the work of an-other imagining, an imagining of what a revolution of/in the now might look like, what might constitute it, fall to the philosopher (a task Jameson and Sloterdikj, each, in their own way, seem ready to take up)? Or the poet or artist? Is the time not now for such a division of labor, born out of the need for a struggle marked by its concurrence and possible convergence? Is that the promise of dual power, a more pointed definition of subreption? That one form of resistance and struggle recognizes its place—its function as a temporary placeholder, as an enabler, if you will, rather than primary agent—in order to finally do away with the corruption that is representative democracy. The athlete and the philosopher or the artist work together, concurrently. However, they proceed along distinct—and, hopefully, complementary—tracks. The first in the service of the second, because it is in and through the second alone that the goal can realized. There is no reason that, say, the artist and the athlete cannot swap places; that is, it is the athlete whose governing logic is utopian—the best of all possible worlds, however, would be for them to be aligned from the beginning.

In this moment, however, the black athletes have gone much further than the poet or the philosopher.

In fact, we can go so far as to say that the black athlete has been sorely underserved by the would-be Leninists. (It is entirely possible that the Leninists, those in our moment who advocate for the strategy of dual power so that we can move beyond reformism, could be birthed out of pure utopian need. Following this, we can then say that it is out of the athletes' absolute need for a new society that a contemporary Leninism may emerge, in whatever guise such a latter-day Leninism may arise.) Poets, artists, philosophers, creative minds of all stripes need to do their work so that the lag in conceptual imagining—one that is free to leave representative democracy far behind—can be redressed. As Jameson suggests, our dystopia may be exactly the moment in which the call for utopian thinking is stronger than it has ever been. Dystopia, as the Icarians, Fourierists, and the Perfectionists well knew, is in dire need of nothing so much as a utopian imaginary.

Only a utopian can save us now.

The athletes have, in truth, freed the artists and the philosophers to imagine to their hearts' content. The work of the black athlete deserves a complementary effort. At the very least.

Undoing dystopia is difficult and laborious, but absolutely necessary, work.

20. From L.A. to Kenosha

I HAD BEEN in the United for less than 4 years, Nip, when I watched the L.A. riots erupt. I watched, mouth agape, live on television, when the officers who had beaten Rodney King to within an inch of his life were found "Not guilty." I will never be able to excise the name "Simi Valley" from my consciousness.

We have now seen how the likes of Rusten Sheskey, if not Derek Chauvin, like so many before them, have history on their side. I fear that there are many more white cops exactly like them. White cops who are empowered by a sense of impunity and, because of that, are but a hair's breath away from unleashing a hail of bullets into yet one more black body. I am at a loss to conclude anything else.

Derek Chauvin convicted. Ma'Khia Bryant shot to death. Andrew Brown gunned down.

From the former U.S. president to the union chiefs such as Bob Kroll, the consistent modality is that power protects its own—and will continue to do, by any means necessary, fair or foul. Power will do whatever it takes to ensure the "rights" of those—its own—who execute and maim black bodies. It is to guard against precisely this predilection that reformism must be stridently opposed. Abolish. Not reform.

Those police officers who, in the dead of night or even under the ubiquitous gaze that is cellphone technology and its capacity to capture the act of violence, consider themselves free to inflict pain and death upon black bodies. These officers know, after all, that history *has taught them this, and they are reminded of it every time one of their own is acquitted across the length and breadth of the nation, that the verdict is always in. One way or another, the outcome is overdetermined. White makes right. Right makes might. Might kills. Black bodies.*

Best to struggle on two fronts, simultaneously, pursuing goals that are finally irreconcilable but necessary. The necessity of the supremacy of a utopian strategy is that it is the surest protection against subreption. The cause, representative democracy, must not be mistaken—as it has so long dissembled—for the solution. Representative democracy is the problem.

In the wake of our intensely dystopic conjuncture, we are presented with a historic opportunity to turn to our utopian imaginary so that we can organize our world as we would want it.

"Enough" is, for all its virtues, for all its eruptive force, for all its ability to galvanize the black athlete, not enough.

Not by itself.

21. Harmolodics

EZRA, *more and more, as a black immigrant of more than three decades standing, as a citizen for a good long while now, I wonder about what exactly it is I am doing here. I am hard-pressed to produce an answer other than it is here, in this country, because of its resources, that I am able to do my work. But I do wonder about the price. Often. In several moments I do not know how to ward off the sheer immensity of the helplessness that overwhelms me. I am bitter to my core. Helpless, as I said, trapped in my inefficacy. I write to keep from dying. At least, I write to you to keep my helplessness in check. I doubt that I succeed to any great degree.*

And so, consider this letter to you as the call for you to think in dual registers. I need you to do this in order that you might, in your own way, be able to imagine the world as you want it to be. I write this letter to you as conceptual map that signposts the limits of representative democracy while not refusing its strategic function.

You are not only an athlete, my son, a thirteen-year old who loves basketball. You are also a musician and a wordsmith. Already you live in many worlds. You practice the guitar, with great reluctance, daily. But always, when you practice, you strive to improvise. Improvisation is how you imagine new styles of dunking.

Does your basketball mindset carry over to your guitar playing? Are they of a piece?

Imagine the radical possibility, to borrow from the philosophical vocabulary of the saxophonist, composer, violinist, and trumpeter Ornette Coleman, that now is the time for "harmolodics." Coleman's harmolodics is that mode of making jazz in which no single musician dominates, in which they all are free to take their imagining as far as they can, building on the playing of those alongside them, improvising ("free jazz" it is also sometimes called) as they feel inspired to, but always, in turn, creating the conditions of maximum possibility for those who will succeed them. For those playing with them.

Nip, you are succeeding several generations.

"Tomorrow," says Coleman, "is the question."

Play, my son, the guitar, basketball, as if you have everything to lose. Because, as you surely intuit, that is the only way to play.

Play as if possessed by the will to answer the "question" that comes from "tomorrow."

Reach for it with all your might.

Acknowledgments

I incurred two debts to my editor, Eric Lundgren, in writing this essay. First, he was instrumental to bringing this project to fruition, and for that I am grateful; and, second, because of Eric's love of music, and jazz in particular, I learned a great deal about Miles Davis, and that was eye-opening in the most enjoyable way.

I am fortunate that Orin Starn and David Andrews, two of the finest minds in sports studies, number among my friends. Orin encouraged me from the start; David provided a generous reading.

Like many, I have long admired Fredric Jameson. His essay "An American Utopia" is central to my thinking in *Only a Black Athlete Can Save Us Now*. I remain, these many years later, honored to have worked with Fred in the Literature Program between 2000 and 2008. Fred is, for me, the definitive example of an intellectual.

Finally, my friend Ian Balfour is a remarkable thinker. I swear, no one knows more about just about everything than Ian. And I do mean everything. From the Pet Shop Boys to David Hume. No one is possessed of a sharper wit. Few are more generous. This one's for you, Professor Balfour.

—GRANT FARRED. *Ithaca, 2020–21*

(Continued from page iii)

Forerunners: Ideas First

Clare Birchall
**Shareveillance: The Dangers of Openly Sharing
and Covertly Collecting Data**

la paperson
A Third University Is Possible

Kelly Oliver
Carceral Humanitarianism: Logics of Refugee Detention

P. David Marshall
The Celebrity Persona Pandemic

Davide Panagia
Ten Theses for an Aesthetics of Politics

David Golumbia
The Politics of Bitcoin: Software as Right-Wing Extremism

Sohail Daulatzai
Fifty Years of *The Battle of Algiers*: Past as Prologue

Gary Hall
The Uberfication of the University

Mark Jarzombek
Digital Stockholm Syndrome in the Post-Ontological Age

N. Adriana Knouf
How Noise Matters to Finance

Andrew Culp
Dark Deleuze

Akira Mizuta Lippit
**Cinema without Reflection: Jacques Derrida's Echopoiesis
and Narcissism Adrift**

Sharon Sliwinski
Mandela's Dark Years: A Political Theory of Dreaming

Grant Farred
Martin Heidegger Saved My Life

Ian Bogost
The Geek's Chihuahua: Living with Apple

Shannon Mattern
Deep Mapping the Media City

Steven Shaviro
No Speed Limit: Three Essays on Accelerationism

Jussi Parikka
The Anthrobscene

Reinhold Martin
Mediators: Aesthetics, Politics, and the City

John Hartigan Jr.
Aesop's Anthropology: A Multispecies Approach

Grant Farred is professor of Africana studies and English at Cornell University and the author of *Martin Heidegger Saved My Life* (Minnesota, 2015), *In Motion, at Rest: The Event of the Athletic Body* (Minnesota, 2014), *What's My Name? Black Vernacular Intellectuals* (Minnesota, 2003), and *Midfielder's Moment: Coloured Literature and Culture in Contemporary South Africa.*